AMBASSADORS OF CHRIST

30 DAILY READINGS FOR RECONCILERS IN AN UNRECONCILED WORLD

PHIL M. WAGLER

Ambassadors Of Christ
Copyright ©2023 Phil Wagler

Published by Castle Quay Books
Burlington, Ontario, Canada and Jupiter, Florida, U.S.A.
416-573-3249 | info@castlequaybooks.com | www.castlequaybooks.com

Edited by Marina Hofman, PhD
Cover design and book interior by Burst Impressions

978-1-998815-04-3 Soft Cover
978-1-998815-05-0 E-book

Library and Archives Canada Cataloguing in Publication
Title: Ambassadors of Christ : 30 daily readings for reconcilers in an unreconciled world / by Phil
    M Wagler.
Names: Wagler, Phil M., author.
Identifiers: Canadiana 20230547966 | ISBN 9781998815043 (softcover)
Subjects: LCSH: Reconciliation—Prayers and devotions. | LCSH: Reconciliation—Religious aspects—
    Christianity. | LCSH: Christian life. | LCSH: Devotional calendars. | LCGFT: Devotional
    literature.
Classification: LCC BV4811 .W33 2023 | DDC 242/.2—dc23

CASTLE QUAY BOOKS

WELCOME TO THE JOURNEY!

PRN Peace &
Reconciliation
Network

A commission of the World Evangelical Alliance (WEA)

The Peace and Reconciliation Network (PRN), a commission of the World Evangelical Alliance, believes every Christian is reconciled to God through Jesus Christ and enlisted in God's mission to reconcile all things to himself. Every Christian is an everyday ambassador of Christ.

The Peace and Reconciliation Network inspires and equips the church and people of peace to enable communities to live life in all its fullness and asks, "What if every local church was a center of reconciliation?" Working with regional and national Evangelical alliances globally, PRN serves to see that peacemaking and the ministry of reconciliation are central to the church's mission everywhere. To learn more or have a PRN leader serve your community, please visit www.reconciledworld.net.

The PRN global team are disciples of the Prince of Peace, just like you. We offer the words below to help you see why being reconcilers in an unreconciled world matters so deeply to us and invite you to journey through these thirty readings prepared by PRN's global director, Phil Wagler.

"Without reconciliation we will not have any meaningful social life in this world."
Johannes Reimer, PRN founder

"Peace and reconciliation as a ministry is usually ignored. I've seen that it's a missing link in the work

of the church and I've stepped forward to be able to occupy that space."
Martin Kapenda, PRN Africa Regional Coordinator

"Reconciliation matters to me first and foremost because it truly in every way matters to God."
Craig Simonian, PRN Caucasus Regional Coordinator

"To me it's important to instill the idea of reconciliation with young people and women because they want to live in peace and in a flourishing way."
Cornelia Reimer, PRN Director of Peacebuilding Education

"God gave us the message to declare that in Jesus's crucifixion and resurrection there is reconciliation with God and each other."
Salim Munayer, PRN Middle East North Africa Regional Coordinator

"The good news of Jesus is not a brand I am promoting or a badge I am wearing. No, the good news is something that is embodied, the way Jesus showed us."
Joel Zantingh, PRN Canada Coordinator

"It is necessary to be reconciled with God, people, and God's creation. This is crucial to me as a follower of Jesus."
Thir Koirala, PRN Asia Regional Coordinator

"People who start seeing Christians taking owner-
ship and pursuing a way for healing open their door
and ask questions for a hope for forgiveness and
reconciliation that only lie in Jesus Christ."
Manuel Boehm, PRN Director of Network
Development

ONE

Ambassadorship Begins with a Call *To* Jesus

On March 11, 2020, a basketball player for the Utah Jazz tested positive for coronavirus. Within days every major professional sports league around the world ceased operation. My ten-year-old bemoaned, "Why does the government take all our fun away!" Everything from the mundane to fun was shaken and stirred in 2020. Sports. Work. School. Home. Zoom. Masks. Church. Politics. Family. Everything.

How do sudden, unexpected events impact you? Do you ask new questions? Do you get exhausted? Do you respond emotionally? Do you lose purpose? Do you seek answers? Do you discover new depths? Life is full of unplanned storms. To survive them, and thrive in them, requires deep spiritual roots.

Jesus calls us to himself to bear spiritual fruit as ambassadors of Christ in this very real world (John 15:5). The Christian spiritual life is ultimately practical, or it is not Christian at all. Jesus said God's kingdom is a seed sprouting toward fruitfulness (Mark 4:26–29). The apostle Paul wrote that life in Christ means being ambassadors of Christ (2 Corinthians 5:18–20).

Spiritual rootedness and growth produce representatives of God's reconciling work in this shaken and broken world. And spiritual growth begins with a summons—a call. Jesus invited people to follow him, the glory of God revealed.

We are called *to* the glory of Jesus. Living as an ambassador of Christ does not begin with a call to behave better or embrace a religious life. Ambassadorship begins with Jesus, who is the glory—the holiness, nature, and beauty of God—revealed in the world.

The disciple John described Jesus as the Word of God made human, a living reality. In Jesus "we have seen God's glory" (John 1:14). Your high call as an ambassador of Christ is contingent on your response to God's word to the world in Jesus Christ.

The call to God's glory in Christ is also a summons to the mission of the Father, Son, and Spirit.

God invites you to come to his glory, so you become his glory in the world (John 17:20–23). This is God's amazing plan in sending Jesus and his purpose in calling you to the glory of Jesus. Your commission as an ambassador of Christ, a reconciler in this unreconciled world, begins with the call of Jesus to center on him.

Is the center of your life the glory of Jesus? If you orbit around the "glory" of anything else, then life is suddenly and shockingly disappointing when an unexpected storm, like a pandemic, interrupts life as we know it. We must assess what we have made the center. Preparation for ambassadors of Christ depends on honesty here.

Your first call is *to* the glory of Jesus—to reorient life around him.

Slow down and consider: Have I given a "yes" or "no" to God's glory revealed in Jesus Christ?

We are never forced, but invited. It is a very personal decision to respond to his summons. His call can come through a friend, scripture, or talk, or the Spirit's quiet urging. His call can come when we are on top of the world or near financial ruin. Regardless, when God's invitation to his glory comes, it will be of the Spirit of God. It will be a spiritual call to live a Spirit-filled and Spirit-formed life in the real world.

This happened to Mary (Luke 1:26–28), Nicodemus (John 3:5–8), Peter (Matthew 16:17), and countless others through history who found true life and holy adventure in response to the call *to* the glory of God revealed in Jesus Christ. The formation of ambassadors of Christ in this very real world begins in the strong whisper of the Divine to come to the glory of Jesus.

Consider yourself summoned.

TWO

AMBASSADORSHIP IS LIFE
FOR THE GLORY OF JESUS

S aul of Tarsus made people suffer. Young and dedicated, he delighted in tracking down Christians to extinguish their affront to the faith of his fathers. Their witness that Jesus was the risen Messiah rankled him (Acts 7:58–8:1; 9:1–3).

He was going to Damascus to bring back followers of "The Way" only to be intercepted by the risen Jesus himself. He was flattened. Blinded by the light, he was led like a toddler to the city. He sat in the dark, refused food or drink, and prayed. His life was about to start again.

God answered. He poked a Christ-follower named Ananias—the type of believer Saul had traveled to Damascus to arrest. God pinned Saul's address on Straight Street and sent Ananias to deliver the answer to his prayers. Saul was to be God's unlikely instrument: the Jewish persecutor of Christians would be God's instrument to proclaim Jesus's name among Gentiles. "I will show him," said the Lord, "how much he must suffer for my name" (Acts 9:16).

The call stuck. Saul—who became Paul and wrote nearly half the New Testament—surrendered his life from this moment for the glory of Jesus. He who had once made others suffer for the name of Jesus answered the call himself.

Paul wrote to the new Christians in the Gentile city of Ephesus: "In him we were also chosen, having been predestined according to the plan of him who works out everything in conformity with the purpose of his will, in order that we, who were the first to put our hope in Christ, might be for the praise of his glory" (Ephesians 1:11–12).

Paul called all Christians to live for Jesus's glory as he was. The communion of saints is called to Jesus—as Paul had been on the highway to Damascus and as you are—to join him in doing God's will in the world. Jesus calls us *to* him to live *for* him.

Life as an ambassador begins in a call to the glory of Jesus. But our ambassadorship sprouts toward fruitfulness— toward a ministry, calling and purpose. We all live for something, even if we aren't aware of it. The Christian is called to live *for* the glory of Jesus. To be reconciled to God in Christ reorients what we live for.

We must ask, "What, or who, am I living for?" Saul had time to process this in Damascus as he sat in the dark. Have you had your dark moment of assessment? Has your church? Anyone, or any community, called *to* Jesus will be led to ask: What, or who, are we living *for*? The Spirit will stir us—and sometimes shake us—with that question. A genuine desire to please God will result in a spiritual confrontation with what, or who, life is for.

Saul believed wholeheartedly that he was living for the right purpose before he met Jesus on that fateful road trip. We too can believe we are doing right and noble things, only to be poked in the eye by the finger of Jesus. Even the right and noble cause can be for self-glory or ethnic or community pride. Jesus will challenge that. He will find a way to have us deeply consider what, or who, we are living for. Ambassadors of reconciliation are awakened by this deep pondering of the soul.

Slow down and consider: "What, or whom, am I living for?" Pray deeply into that question. How has Jesus been getting your attention and exposing the "What for?" of your life? The ambassadorial impact of your life toward the reconciling purposes of God depends on your honest answer.

THREE

Ambassadorship Grows
WITH the Glory of Jesus

We grow better with others. Being with others makes us better.

The Kohler effect, named for psychologist Otto Kohler in the 1920s, describes a human reality: we are more highly motivated in groups than when we try to go it alone. This is instructive, given that "I can do it myself!" and "I want what I want!" seem to be the chief motives of the twenty-first century human—especially as defined from the western world. Individualism is celebrated and elevated, but ironically that doesn't help us grow as healthy people.

Conversely, we can even look on our people group or ethnic tribe individually and believe we can do life without others who are different from us as well. Even communal thinking can be ironically individualized.

These sociological truths confirm the image of God we bear. Christians confess the mystery that God is One in community. There is one God, revealed as Father, Son, and Spirit. Jesus lived his life on the way to the cross and resurrection from the source of divine oneness. He prayed for us to live from this source too: "that they may be one, just as you, Father, are in me, and I in you, that they also may be in us, so that the world may believe that you sent me" (John 17:21).

Jesus hopes for us to know the same "oneness" with the Father that he has. This community in communion is God's divine nature and his desire for his people, who will be his community of ambassadors.

Jesus's prayer continues with a stupendous thought: "The glory that you have given me I have given to them, that they may be one even as we are one" (John 17:22). The community of disciples are not only called *to* the glory of Jesus and *for* the glory of Jesus but *are* the glory of Jesus in the world. Christians are the diverse yet unified expression of the oneness of Father, Son, and Spirit. Jesus's followers in fellowship, contending for the unity of the Spirit (Ephesians 4:3), mutually in submission to one another (Ephesians 5:21), become God's glory, his reflection and beauty in an individualistic, conflicted, me-first or us-first world. Jesus's church is to be the glory of Jesus (Ephesians 3:21).

This great mystery has a very simple implication: Christian ambassadorship is never done alone. Growing up in Christ and his call can include solitude, but it is no solitary venture. We grow *with* his glory: *with* his church. We are growing with others into the likeness and fullness of Christ (Ephesians 4:13). In fact, we *need* others to grow—as the Kohler effect demonstrates. If God himself is community, and we are made in the image of God, we will also need community. To think we can grow into effective ambassadorship otherwise is a fallacy.

Slow down and consider: Where are you at in relationship to other Christians? Are you *with* Jesus's glory, his church? You won't grow into the character and nature of God—a communion of oneness—without others. Neither will your church fellowship grow into its ambassadorial effectiveness without other churches.

Who really knows you, is spurring you on, sharpening your iron, calling you to the Good News life, rebuking what needs correcting, teaching you how to reconcile and be reconciled, sending you on mission, loving you, and naming your gifts?

After you've assessed that, move in one of two directions. If you're going alone, take an intentional step to walk more closely with other disciples. This can take courage, but don't wait for someone else to make the first move. Spiritual growth is not their responsibility, it's yours.

If, however, you're loving the mutuality of the communion of the saints, take an intentional step to come alongside someone who needs to get *with* the glory of Jesus. Pray and ask the Spirit to show you someone riding alone. Then, don't let them stay that way.

FOUR

Ambassadorship Is Life
BY THE GLORY OF JESUS

How many social media platforms are you on? In this age of self-promotion, updating our profiles to stand out from the crowd can be a full-time job. Conversely, this is also an age where the pressure to conform to the latest trend or cause is immense. This tension between unique self-promotion and conforming to group identity is costly, tenuous, and unsettling to the soul. Am I led by my need to be a "successful" individual or by my need to fit into the crowd? This can be paralyzing or imprisoning.

Jesus lived with clarity. He knew what and who he was led by. "My food is to do the will of him who sent me, and to finish his work" (John 4:34). "For I have come down from heaven, not to do my own will, but the will of him who sent me" (John 6:38). Invite me into your life story, he says, because "whoever welcomes me does not welcome me but the one who sent me" (Mark 9:37). And when he could have most naturally succumbed to ego or pressure, he surrendered to the Father: "not my will, but yours be done" (Luke 22:42).

Jesus was led *by* God's glory. His coming was all by the Father's initiative, and he rested in that clarity. Jesus had a peace that disturbed precisely because he knew who he was led by. He who was God's glory revealed was constantly led by God's glory.

This is God's intention for all his ambassadors. The Israelites were led by God's glory in a pillar of fire and cloud during their exodus from Egypt (Exodus 13:21). The glory of God led Isaiah to his moment of surrender; "Here I am Lord, send me" (Isaiah 6:8). Jesus called his first disciples to a higher glory, from fishermen to fishers of men (Matthew 4:19). Even the disturbing realities of this broken world— like why a man was born blind—are reframed by the glory of God (John 9). The coming of the Holy Spirit brings God's glory into every repentant heart, leading into truth and righteousness (John 16:13). The Spirit leads the church to participate in God's mission in the world for the glory of God. The Spirit empowers Christians to offer their gifts so that the church may shine as the body of Christ, God's glory revealed. In short, everything God is doing in the world is led by his glory, led by the glory centered in Jesus Christ.

Our ambassadorship begins with a call *to* the glory of Jesus. Then, we surrender our lives *for* the glory of Jesus. We grow best in the context of community, the body of Christ, where we are *with* the glory of Jesus. And we step into our purpose as we are led *by* the glory of Jesus. It is not our ego or conforming to the crowd that moves us into our part in God's reconciling work in the world; it is *by* the glory of Jesus that our fishing, plumbing, teaching, farming, pastoring, nursing, parenting, banking, or whatever else moves to its higher, God-intended purpose.

Slow down and consider: what is my life led by? Is it ego or the crowd?

Ambassadors of Christ must be led from nowhere else and for no other purpose. Think of it with this baseball metaphor: it's as if you're standing on third base—having been called *to*, *for*, and *with* the glory of Jesus—and Jesus is the cleanup hitter. He is the one who drives you home. It is *by* him that you are driven you're your meaningful—even if seemingly small—contribution in the reconciling mission of God.

Is my life led by the glory of Jesus? Where has he placed me or my people by his glory to be his ambassador?

FIVE

ALL THIS IS FROM GOD...

Our family vehicle died. It was undriveable. The cost was enormous to fix and beyond its worth. And this was all happening shortly after I had lost a job and just days before Christmas. How were we going to transport our family of eight?

Into that mess and confusion stepped friends—including people I didn't even know—who pooled together money to help our family get into a reliable vehicle. Every time I sat behind the wheel of that family van, I was reminded that all this is a gift. All this is an act of grace, love, and kindness.

In 2 Corinthians 5:18 the apostle Paul says, "All this is from God, who reconciled us to himself through Christ and gave us the ministry of reconciliation." We will dive into this entire verse as it relates to our calling to ambassadorship over the next few readings. We begin with the first five words: "All this is from God..."

Paul is uncovering the wonder of God's reconciling love and grace. The call to, for, with, and by Jesus brings the surrendered life into a new world, a new creation (2 Corinthians 5:17).

In other words, the way of looking at the world is completely renewed. Christians see the world through new glasses—actually, through whole new eyes! Paul understood precisely what this was like from his own transformative experience. To use the metaphor of my new family vehicle:

how I see driving is transformed by the awareness that "all this" was unmerited love and gift.

For the growing ambassador of Christ, the world is brand new because of Jesus and the reconciling work of God, even as we live in the world we've always inhabited. In 2 Corinthians Paul is revealing his own conviction of what being Christ's ambassador means—his own process of learning to wear the lenses of God's kingdom. The "all this" that he is now aware of includes how he sees others (5:16), what he lives for (5:15), what controls him (5:14), his calling and purpose (5:11), what his life aim is (5:9), and how he even sees challenges and opposition (5:6; 4:16–18).

As we grow into our "new eyes," we become increasingly aware that we have been given "all this" from God: a new position as children of God and new perspective on what is ultimate reality. And "all this" is only possible because God has loved and graced us with his reconciling work in Jesus Christ. "All this" is because of Jesus's incarnation and his proclamation and demonstration of God's good-news reign in his teachings, miracles, suffering, death, resurrection, and ascension.

Slow down and consider: How are you seeing the world? How do you see others? What are you living for? What controls you? What's your purpose? How do you face challenges and opposition? As a disciple you are literally a new creation and gifted to see yourself and the world anew. It's all grace. You're driving a car you should not have, yet there you are behind the wheel looking through a whole new glass because God has made the impossible possible.

How does this become practical for you? What does "all this" mean for the way you will live in your world, relationships, and responsibilities today? What does "all this" mean for the fellowship of disciples that you are traveling with?

SIX

WHO THROUGH CHRIST HAS RECONCILED US TO HIMSELF...

I have read volumes and watched many movies about the Great (in the most horrible sense of the word) Wars of the twentieth century. The First World War was even dubbed, most inaccurately, "the war to end war" by H. G. Wells in 1914. In my homeland, Canada, we pause on November 11 to remember the armistice of World War I. For a few moments we stop to acknowledge suffering, courage, and destructive nationalism.

Sadly, however, on that day, we're remembering armistice, and armistice is not the end of war; it's only a halt to hostilities while everyone tries to negotiate a more persevering peace. Essentially, Remembrance Day in my country is a commemoration of our human desire for cease-fire, but our tragic incapacity to keep it. Humanity is still seeking a lasting peace.

The Bible is the great (in the most wonderful sense of the word) story of the accomplished lasting peace between God and humanity. This lasting peace can change everything— from internal personal conflicts to friendships and marriages, work and play, how peoples relate to one another, and how humanity will steward creation.

Humanity lives at war with God. We resist his commands. We reject his wooing. We mock his ways. We resist personal relationship. Yet, despite this cataclysmic broken relationship, the good news is that through Christ God has reconciled us to himself. "All this is from God," writes the apostle Paul, "who reconciled us to himself through Christ" (2 Corinthians 5:18).

Christian ambassadors live the consequences of no longer being at war with God. We are not simply living with a cessation of hostilities but resting in the wonder that "since we have been justified by faith, we have peace with God through our Lord Jesus Christ" (Romans 5:1).

In Jesus Christ's appearance, life, teaching, miracles, death, resurrection, and ascension, God has done all that was needed to not simply stop the shooting, but to fully make us his own family with all rights, privileges, and ambassadorial responsibilities. To use the national battles that still rage as a metaphor, it's as if Iranians have adopted Americans as full brothers and sisters or as if those on the political right have fully welcomed in those on the left as their very own. That seems impossible and almost absurd, doesn't it?

And yet, this is what is true for Christians: we who were enemies are brought near by the blood of Christ (Colossians 1:21; Ephesians 2:13). There is no armistice to negotiate: the war is over. Period. Lasting peace has come. While we were still firing our weapons and sharpening our spears, God reconciled us to himself through Jesus Christ. When Jesus went to the cross, the battle ended. Your war is over.

Slow down and consider: Are you still at war with God? Are you trying to prove yourself? Are you determined to do things your way? Are you doubting the truth of what he says about your sin, resistance, need for repentance and new life?

25

Are you arguing with him about what his Word says about who you are as a child of God?

When we strive against God, we're acting as if all we can hope for is armistice, when the good news is that through Christ God has reconciled us to himself. Lasting peace has been accomplished. It is finished.

What might change deep down if you accepted this lasting peace? If you realized that you are fully reconciled and fully at peace, what might change and awaken in your spirit? What might that mean for the world you are in today?

SEVEN

WE ARE GIVEN THE MINISTRY OF RECONCILIATION

I was in Eastern Europe and needed local cash. My friend took me to the back of a jewelry store, of all places, where I passed American dollars through a small window to someone I could barely see. It was a strange experience for a North American who normally entered a bank for such transactions. Yet soon I was passed a stack of the new currency to use—presumably to immediately buy jewelry!

Our great God has completed *the* great exchange. Through Jesus Christ we are reconciled to God. This is the best of news. God has exchanged the enmity and brokenness that shaped our relationship with him because of sin for the lasting peace of adoption into the family of God (Romans 8:15). We are children of God through faith in Jesus Christ, who laid down his life for his enemies (Romans 5:10; John 1:12; Galatians 3:26). We are now God's friends and family.

To be reconciled is to exchange one reality for another. The Greek word *katallasso* (translated "reconciled" in English) was originally used for the exchange of coins or money and then evolved to express the exchange of one reality for a new one (like singleness for marriage or warring for friendship). In other words, you exchanged one currency for another as if you have entered a new land altogether. When we surrender our lives to Jesus, we become the inhabitants of a new creation (2 Corinthians 5:17), and the old cash simply doesn't work anymore. It has, in fact, been exchanged for something new entirely. God himself was the mysterious figure who made this new reality possible.

But it gets even better!

As a result of this lasting peace with God (Romans 5:1), we have also been given a ministry, the ministry of exchange. We are given the gift and privilege of participating in God's work of reconciling the world to himself. Having the spiritual identity of the reconciled, God now gives to the reconciled the ministry of reconciliation (2 Corinthians 5:18). We join him as currency exchangers in the world. We become "ambassadors for Christ" (2 Corinthians 5:20), the people through whom God is revealing his will and imploring the world to his great exchange and his ways, character, and fruit.

Ambassadors of Christ embrace the full reality and privilege of this exchange. On one side of the reconciled coin, we have a new identity and standing with God. On the other side, we have a ministry to be about in the world. We are now reconciled *and* reconcilers. We are exchanged *and* exchangers.

Slow down and consider: Where has God placed you? There are likely great exchanges necessary all around. Perhaps co-workers or friends are at odds. Perhaps enmity and strife swirl in your home or neighbourhood. Perhaps political discourse or ideologies are dividing and fracturing rather than building a common good. Christ's ambassadors are the reconciled, and the reconciled have the ministry of reconciliation to be about wherever there is opportunity.

Is there a place, a relationship, or a situation that the Holy Spirit is opening your eyes to see with new clarity? How will you become a reconciler there? How can you be an ambassador of the great exchange?

EIGHT

THIRSTY FOR LIFE

On a sweltering summer day, we went to a park for a family baseball game. Parents versus kids. A summer classic. It didn't take long for the old folks to twist ankles and tweak muscles. We persevered, sweated, and thirsted. It was so excruciatingly hot that our son ended up with heat stroke.

He was so caught up in the game that he didn't replenish, and it left him in rough shape. We drove quickly for fluid, and he downed two electrolyte-laden drinks in short order. The result of the game suddenly became secondary to what his body craved.

Are you thirsty? What do you thirst for?

Jesus's conversation with the Samaritan woman in Sychar is built around thirst. Seated by a well in the heat of the day, Jesus presses the troubled woman who is longing for more from life: "If you knew the gift of God, and who it is that is saying to you, 'Give me a drink,' you would have asked him, and he would have given you living water" (John 4:10). She is stunned that Jesus knows her real, deeper thirst and presents himself as the answer.

At the Jewish Feast of Booths, when vessels of water were poured out representing the giving of the Law and a sign of the promised outpouring of the Spirit of God, Jesus declared, "If anyone thirsts, let him come to me and drink. Whoever believes in me, as the Scripture has said, 'Out of his heart will flow rivers of living water'" (John 7:37–39). Jesus centers the deep, hopeful thirst of the Jewish nation in himself.

To the Samaritan Jesus gives the promise that the Gentile thirst will be quenched. To the Jews, who were to be ambassadors of hope for the nations (Isaiah 2:1–5), Jesus declares that the satisfying of their deep ethnic thirst will produce living water for a thirsty world.

To be an ambassador of Christ (2 Corinthians 5:18–20) requires a thirst for true life. We are gifted the ministry of reconciliation in a world riddled with pain, division, chaos, and conflict. It's hot out there! What is quenching your thirst? Are you aware of how thirsty you must be?

Jesus's interactions in Sychar and Jerusalem (see Matthew 11:28–30) show how we access this living water he is and brings: we need to admit our thirst and come to him. The ambassadorial call we have is immense; if we don't admit our thirst and keep coming to him, the heat will overwhelm and bake us.

Slow down and consider: What is your deepest thirst? Are you aware of your calling and context? Are you aware of the heat? Are you just pressing on, or are you admitting your thirst and need for a deep well of living water to constantly draw from? Are you coming to Jesus regularly, seeking his word of life and the filling of the Holy Spirit? Without this thirst for true life, you will wilt as an ambassador of Christ.

Do the work of the Samaritan: assess your life and admit your thirst. What list of things is depleting and running you dry? What hidden realities have parched you, alienated you from others, and left you panting?

Do the work of the Jews in Jerusalem: discipline yourself to come with your thirst to the place where it can be met. What practices of coming to Jesus are yours regularly so that living water flows from you to the world in which you are an ambassador of Christ, the living water?

NINE

AMBASSADORS OF CHRIST: POOR IN SPIRIT

I recall the patched together home of a mom and her sons in a Chilean *campamento*. Dirt floors. Salvaged wood walls. Corrugated tin roof. Tattered sheets hung to create "rooms." We were visiting because one of her sons was brilliant but in dire need of financial help for education. His abilities could rescue his family from poverty, but he had no capacity to get the training. This was a most unjust poverty. The family confessed an entrapped powerlessness.

Jesus begins training his ambassadors in Matthew with curious words: "Blessed are the poor in spirit, for theirs is the kingdom of heaven" (Matthew 5:3). Those Jesus called to follow him (Matthew 4:19) were to possess what is of greatest worth—the kingdom of heaven—through a settled condition of poverty they were to be happy about it ("blessed" in the original Greek means happy or enviable)!

Ambassadors of God's kingdom are discovered below the poverty line. Luke's version of the same words Matthew records have a slight tonal difference, "Blessed are you who are poor, for yours is the kingdom of God" (Luke 6:20). The powerlessness of poverty is debilitating, awakens desperation, and clarifies what is of greatest value. It's a curious descriptor for ambassadors of the Lord of glory; yet being "poor" seems to be a prerequisite for discovering true riches.

Combined, the two biblical writers underline a crucial point: the poor have an advantage and the advantaged are poor. The Scriptures force us to wrestle with this truth at both a spiritual and sociological level. Disciples of Jesus must wrestle with the tension and overlap of the spiritual and material, of heaven and earth.

There is nothing holy in material poverty, but material riches are a bait and switch—you can gain the whole world and lose your soul (Matthew 16:26). There is no buying, earning, or hedge-funding your way into a position of royalty in God's kingdom, but it does seem riches can get you into Satan's dominion (Luke 16:19–31). The kingdom belongs to the poor and the poor in spirit. These are the two sides of the currency of the kingdom of heaven. In God's economy the awareness of need and want are where it all begins.

The old preacher, John Chrysostom (c. 347–407), cried, "The greatest of evils, and those which make havoc of the whole world, had their entering in from pride." Pride is the opposite of poverty of spirit. Pride is the great and bitter root of sin. Pride destroys and wreaks havoc. Pride earns, gathers, and parades its accomplishments and possessions. Pride demands, it never confesses.

Ambassadorship is not for the proud. The proud build their empires. Ambassadors, on the other hand, always represent another kingdom. Their position and power come entirely from somewhere else.

Ambassadors of Christ possess everything precisely because they are aware of their dependency. Through the prophet Isaiah, the LORD declared,

For this is what the high and exalted One says—

he who lives forever, whose name is holy:

"I live in a high and holy place,

but also with the one who is contrite and lowly
in spirit,

to revive the spirit of the lowly

and to revive the heart of the contrite."

(Isaiah 57:15)

The LORD grounds his ambassadors in a rich paradox: a lowliness, a below-the poverty-line life that possesses everything and empowers a positional and ambassadorial life in a world where pride runs wild.

Visiting that Chilean family reoriented me. The smell and experience of poverty will do that to the privileged, but only to the extent that it awakens awareness of one's own poverty. Spiritual poverty is the common ground of rich and poor alike; it's just that the materially poor seem to arrive there first and have a way of pointing the rest of the world to what is of ultimate worth.

Slow down and consider: Where is this tension of below-the-poverty-line life true for you? What do you believe is true riches? What does an audit of your spirit reveal? Do you possess the kingdom Jesus says you can, or has pride duped you into laying claim to an inferior standing?

Do some spiritual accounting, and do some sacrificing with King David—who possessed a vast earthly kingdom:

"My sacrifice, O God, is a broken spirit;

a broken and contrite heart

you, God, will not despise." (Psalm 51:17)

This, wealthy David knew, is the path to true riches and ambassadorship in the everlasting kingdom.

TEN

AMBASSADORS OF CHRIST: THOSE WHO MOURN

C an you recall the first time you saw a parent cry?
I have an enduring image of my usually stoic dad breaking down in tears at my grandparents' farm when I was about ten years old. It was confusing. It shifted my understanding of him. That moment lingered in my mind's file folder for years because I never knew what caused the outburst. Only just before his death did I have the courage to ask about that childhood moment when I saw my dad weep.

One of the first images we have of God in Scripture is of a pained heart. With the wickedness of humanity spreading virally we see a holy God who "was grieved in his heart" (Genesis 6:6). The brokenness of his world touches God deeply and moves him to action. God is hurt and shows it.

Jesus's training of his kingdom ambassadors includes this heavenly invitation: "Blessed are those who mourn, for they shall be comforted" (Matthew 5:4). "Blessed," of course, literally means happy or enviable. Jesus is calling his ambassadors to the happy life of mourning. He is inviting us to the God-like life.

This godliness is vividly revealed in two other Gospel accounts. The first is the shocking portrayal of the father in the parable of the Lost Son—a story of two wayward sons and a father who loves deeply (Luke 15:11–32). The power of the parable is as much in what is unsaid as in what is said.

The father feels the pain of rejection, broken relationship, the agony of waiting, and the disappointment of having his children miss the point. Jesus presents God the Father as gentle and strong, as persevering through pain.

The other Gospel account is the death of Jesus's friend Lazarus. John—present when "Blessed are those who mourn" was first spoken—summarizes what he saw in just two words: "Jesus wept" (John 11:35). Mourning over the brokenness of the world is not a doctrinal position for God; it is real and personal. God is deeply moved and is moved to action.

When Jesus describes the blessing of mourning and the promise of comfort, he is inviting us to see and experience the world as God does and receive the comfort God alone is. In fact, "Comforter" is a descriptor of the Holy Spirit (John 15:26).

To share our heavenly Father's pain for this broken world is a blessed and enviable privilege, for it is a sign we have finally come spiritually alive and will receive the comfort God himself provides. It is blessing and sweet, ironic comfort to experience the heartache of God.

Slow down and consider: What grieves you? Who makes you cry? Does the world's brokenness grieve you? Do you even notice it, or has your heart grown calloused? Have you experienced the tears that lead to God's hopeful comfort? Has grief crippled you or moved you to action? And if none of this is true for you, why not?

Many live far too long with their heavenly Father being a mystery like my dad was to me. My dad and I eventually got to the root of his tears, and it filled a gap for me that made my love for him grow. We don't need to wait to understand our Father in heaven. From the Bible's beginnings to the full revelation of God in Jesus Christ, we know a God who mourns and acts to bring this sad world comfort. This is our King. We are his mournful ambassadors.

How are you being moved to see your world, pray for your world, act into your world as one who mourns? What might require unblocking in your own story to get there? How is the Comforter inviting you to know the heart of God more fully so you can represent him as heaven's ambassador?

ELEVEN

AMBASSADORS OF CHRIST: THE MEEK

A college hockey team I coached went on an exhibition tour of a European country. For the most part we got completely clobbered. In one city we visited an orphanage where the young men on my team transformed before my eyes as brawny twenty-year-old athletes cuddled and played with precious abandoned babies and toddlers. The tough competitors were suddenly tender warriors holding the vulnerable in their strong hands.

"Blessed are the meek, for they will inherit the earth" (Matthew 5:5).

Jesus is forming a team of ambassadors; agents of another world in this one. He describes them as enviable and happy in their meekness. Later in Matthew, Jesus describes himself this way: "Take my yoke upon you and learn from me, for I am gentle and humble in heart, and you will find rest for your souls" (Matthew 11:29). (The Greek word here translated "gentle" is *praus,* the same as "meek" in Matthew 5:5, only translated with a different nuance.)

What is this meekness? Does it sound like weakness to you? And how will ambassadors of meekness ever make a discernible difference in this tough world? Don't we need more who aggressively crash the corners and put the earth in its place?

Jesus, counterculturally, is elevating not bravado or power as the world assumes, but the harnessed strength of those who hold the vulnerable. "Meekness," as Jesus speaks it, is as far from weakness as my college hockey team was from the Stanley Cup. *Praus* refers to the exercising of great strength under great control. God's power under God's control. It is power without abuse, authority without harshness, influence without demanding rights.

Meekness is, as Palestinian church leader Elias Chacour describes, "not weakness but relying fully on God's power as Moses had."

Moses began his life acting like a goon. He had a passion for justice and even killed justifiably. Moses's strength needed harnessing. He needed God's power and restraint. That is what he learned in the wilderness of exile, before a burning bush, and in depending entirely on God's presence and promises in the courts of Pharaoh.

David learned this too. His bravery before Goliath and popularity needed to be harnessed by God. His passion for Israel and his struggle with Saul the flailing king all needed to become meek. He needed his anointed authority harnessed in utter dependence on God. David came to know that meekness the Spirit of God alone forms: a humility and lowliness that is unleashed in transformative power.

When Jesus calls the meek "blessed," he echoes King David in Psalm 37. There David says do not fret, trust the LORD and do good, commit your way to the LORD, be still before the LORD, refrain from anger, and, essentially, be harnessed by God's presence and promises. Meekness is not weakness, but a life harnessed to God when all is uncertain and seems lost and you just want to rage. David writes, "The meek will inherit the land and enjoy peace and prosperity" (Psalm 37:11).

Jesus calls his ambassadors to this strong, surrendered life under the control of God. The meek renounce every right of their own and inherit what everyone seeks. It is to these blessed and enviable ones that God entrusts his shalom on earth. (*Shalom* is the Hebrew word translated as "peace," "well-being," or even "prosperity" in English and communicates wholeness and God's very best for his creation.) Isn't this precisely what God himself did when, in Christ, he harnessed his power to the cross to reconcile us to himself?

Slow down and consider: Where are you moved to passionate action? Where are you ready to exert strength for a well-intentioned good? Then ask, are you harnessed to true power as you go there? Are you acting like Moses before his wilderness training? Or are you learning the lessons of the meek King, fully surrendered to God's power and harnessed by his presence and promises precisely because the earth is a violent and violated mess? Are you holding the earth's vulnerability and fragility in hands held by the gentle strength of the Divine?

The authority of ambassadors of Christ is not in our rights, but in leaving our rights to God alone. This meekness reveals that we come as ambassadors carrying a citizenship that is not of this world, but immensely powerful in it.

TWELVE

AMBASSADORS OF CHRIST: THE HUNGRY AND THIRSTY

I remember the first time I tasted the wonder of shrimp as a boy. I had no idea such succulence existed. And that sauce to dip it in! Oh my! That first experience didn't end my journey with this savoury seafood, it merely awakened a hunger for more.

> Taste and see that the LORD is good;
>> blessed is the one who takes refuge in him.
>
> (Psalm 34:8)

This poetry of Scripture invites us to a first taste. Like those sample tables in grocery stores, God invites you to taste and see—not so you can be satisfied with having tried him, but to awaken you to a whole new world, much like I experienced when I tasted shrimp for the first time. God wants to whet our appetite, so we yearn for more and more of his righteousness, of what gets his seal of approval in the world.

The biblical prophets saw righteousness as active and tangible. To know the Holy, Righteous One was to hunger and thirst for his righteousness in the world. The absence of what was right in God's sight was proof that the righteousness and goodness of the LORD had not been tried. Human beings then, and now, often rushed into impulse purchases of the world and its sinful brokenness with unsurprisingly disastrous desserts: "So justice is far from us, and righteousness does not reach us" (Isaiah 59:9).

Proverbs 30:15–16 describes life that is true to our experience,

> The leech has two daughters.
> "Give! Give!" they cry.
> There are three things that are never satisfied,
> four that never say, "Enough!":
> the grave, the barren womb,
> land, which is never satisfied with water,
> and fire, which never says, "Enough!"

We are all faced with a critical choice: will we be leeches who cry "gimme, gimme" but never become satisfied, or will we hunger and thirst for more and more of what truly fulfills? We were not created to leech! The Lord's invitation is to a hunger and thirst that *is* satisfied and *brings* satisfaction to the deep hunger of the world.

Jesus builds his ambassadorial force declaring, "Blessed are those who hunger and thirst for righteousness, for they will be filled" (Matthew 5:6).

The ambassador of Christ is freely and joyfully aware that righteousness is provided only by the Lord. Tasting, hungering, and thirsting for more and more and more of God is the only hope for righteousness. God the Righteous One is discovered on the journey of following and obeying him where we taste and see that God is the ultimate good and true satisfaction. "Those who follow Jesus," writes Dietrich Bonhoeffer in *The Cost of Discipleship*, "grow hungry and thirsty on the way."

Those who hunger and thirst for more of who God is and what he is about in the world will be filled as their taste is awakened. Only as we go on the trail with Jesus, seek justice, and do that which the prophets decried was missing does a holy hunger and thirst emerge. Rising and going with Jesus is the way to the fuller satisfaction of what we taste-tested and discovered a greater hunger for.

Slow down and consider: What are you hungry for? What pangs have you fed in life that, like the leaping flames, have never said "Enough?" Have you tasted and seen that the Lord is good? Can you recall even the smallest taste-test of God's righteousness? Did you leave lesser things behind for more of that true satisfaction?

Now, what are you going to do about it? Where might you taste-test God's justice and righteousness in your relationships, workplace, and anywhere else you have influence and ambassadorial responsibility? Taste and see. Hunger and thirst for God's righteousness; you will be filled.

THIRTEEN

AMBASSADORS OF CHRIST: THE MERCIFUL

Amon Goethe, the Nazi concentration camp comman-
dant in the film *Schindler's List*, is a brute. He kills
willingly. He lacks empathy. He seeks power. Oskar Schindler, who is covertly rescuing Jews as a business owner,
attempts to influence Goethe by planting seeds of mercy.

In a fascinating scene, Schindler and Goethe discuss the
power to kill. Schindler turns the idea of power on its head
using a parable, contending for a truer power, "That's what
the emperors had. A man stole something, he's brought in
before the emperor, he throws himself down on the ground,
he begs for mercy, he *knows* he's going to die. And the
emperor pardons him. This worthless man, he lets him go."
Goethe thinks this is madness, that his compatriot is drunk.

"No," says Schindler, "that's power, Amon. That is power."

Schindler's tale echoes Jesus's parable of the unmerciful
servant (Matthew 18:21–35). There a servant owes an
exorbitant amount, a debt worthy of imprisonment or worse,
but the master has mercy. Shockingly, that servant, having
received mercy, immediately refuses similar compassion to
someone owing him a very small debt. The master is furious:
"Shouldn't you have had mercy on your fellow servant just
as I had on you?" (Matthew 18:33). The parable is jarring,
but Jesus is highlighting the character of God that should
become the character of his ambassadors.

The great sin of Israel following their deliverance from Egypt was a golden calf they credited for their liberty (Exodus 32:4). The LORD is justifiably angry. He's ready to destroy the ungrateful nation and start over. Moses stands in the gap, intercedes, declares the covenant-keeping character of God and begs the LORD not to abandon his people. The LORD, faithful to himself, tells Moses that he will make all his goodness pass in front of Moses, a revelation of the divine nature. The LORD overwhelms Moses with his presence, proclaiming: "The LORD, the LORD, a God merciful and gracious, slow to anger, and abounding in steadfast love and faithfulness" (Exodus 34:6).

The powerful presence of the LORD, following a great rebellion, comes with the declaration of his mercy. The LORD is the master showing mercy toward great debtors. Mercy for the pitiful—this is power. Those who receive undeserved mercy, who know the God of mercy, are to share this power.

Jesus's ambassadors are showered in mercy. "Blessed are the merciful, for they will be shown mercy" (Matthew 5:7).

Enviable and happy are the merciful. God must be very happy. We should desire his joy and revel in mercy with him. Jesus, assuming his hearers know the revelation of the LORD to Moses, instructs his disciples to join in God's powerful mercy. To be merciful is to be God-like. Ambassadors of Christ are mercenaries of mercy. When we are merciful, we receive the joy of mercy too.

There is one more serious consideration. Mercy is not something God does as one part of his holy job description; it is who the LORD *is*. Mercy is God's nature and character.

Mercy is to become his ambassadors. Ambassadors of Christ are compassionate because they are becoming like God.

What is the opposite of merciful? Cruel. Unforgiving. Harsh. Unkind. Ungiving. Amon Goethe.

The test of whether mercy is us is not whether we want it or even know we need it. It's whether it shows up when we are rejected and despised, as the LORD was by the Israelites and their golden calf. Does mercy show up when the pitiful and pitied are in my grip? It is sobering that, like the servant before the merciful master, mercy received is no guarantee that we give the gift ourselves.

Slow down and consider: What has God done with your massive debt? How do you respond when you are sinned against, offended, despised, and rejected? How deep is the awareness of the mercy you have received? How empathetic is your awareness of the mercy others need? Where do you see harshness and unforgiveness abounding? This world needs the power of the merciful. Now, what are you going to do about it?

FOURTEEN

AMBASSADORS OF CHRIST: THE PURE IN HEART

Anyone who works in the not-for-profit world knows the adventure of faith and knows how amazing it is to see God provide through people's sacrificial generosity. I have grown much as I learn dependence on the Lord and humble partnership with others. And it has a way of exposing my impurity.

I disturb me. I am troubled that I can talk with someone—even a friend—hear life's challenges and joys, share the adventures of my own soul and the work of God, and *still* wonder how I could convince them to give money to the cause. This impurity unsettles me. I desire for God to form in me an unmixed heart.

"Blessed are the pure in heart, for they shall see God" (Matthew 5:8).

Jesus's ambassadors are to know the enviable quality of an unmixed heart. "Purity" means without additives or mixture and free from contamination. It's what we want when we thirst for "pure water" or hunger for food with no preservatives. It's like honey: 100 per cent pure!

In the Old Testament, God could only be approached by the pure. The Law given to Israel detailed requirements for ritual purity. Elaborate processes dealt with very normal life situations that brought impurity, such as touching a sick or dead body, menstrual cycles, and even certain foods.

Israelite priests followed strict guidelines to approach God in the temple. An unclean priest could literally die (like Nadab and Abihu did in Leviticus 10).

The point wasn't that people needed to be perfect, but that the LORD is perfect. It's not that God *didn't* want humans to approach his splendour; it's precisely that he *did* want them to enjoy him. God is ultimately consistent and without mixture. He is pure.

"The words of the LORD are pure words" says Psalm 12:6. God's speech comes from a pure heart. God's intent and purpose are always consistent with his goodness and holiness. There is no bait and switch with God. In God there is no manipulation or exploitation. His words are pure because he is pure. God's love is not mixed with ulterior motives. The anger of God is not mixed with malice.

You can trust purity. In fact, God's pure love for the world and wrath against sin will make us pure (1 Corinthians 1:30). God can miraculously extract the impurities that have found their way into our heart, soul, mind, and strength and have corrupted love for God, neighbour, and self. And to the pure God will reveal himself. They will see God.

When Jesus says, "Blessed are the pure in heart," he is calling us to the enviable life found only in God, in order that we might be enviable in a world longing for purity. The world needs purity. The world needs to see God. Jesus is raising up an ambassadorial force of the pure who long to and will see God. And if we see God, we will see and embrace life in this mixed-up world with the purity he does (2 Corinthians 5:16).

Slow down and consider: Do you know what it feels like to work with, live with, or befriend someone with mixed motives, purposes, intentions, and words? Impurity destroys what is beautiful and best. Where do you see this in the world? Do you see it in yourself? Don't you long to see God? Don't you long for the world to see the absolute purity of the Lord?

Our impurity must be resolved, but how does one achieve purity of heart? Can impure water cleanse itself? This miracle God alone can do—like turning water into wine. In the Old Testament, God made a way for the impure to approach God. Now, in Christ, God has made us pure through the ritual and sacrificial purity of his Son. Purity of heart comes, ironically, from confessing our impurity. Our contaminated hearts can be transformed by the One who is pure. God's purity will then be seen by and in his ambassadors too.

FIFTEEN

AMBASSADORS OF CHRIST: THE PEACEMAKERS

B lessed are the peacemakers, for they will be called children of God" (Matthew 5:9).

My wife and I have six kids. I know a peace that has been shattered. When the peace is ripped apart by warring siblings or irritated parents, it's sometimes necessary to get some space. That is peacekeeping.

Peace*making* is harder. "Go to your room!" and you can happily wallow in self-justifying self-pity, feed your offense, or just bury the moment. The real work is bringing the angry and wounded together, see each other's eyes, own our part, forgive, receive forgiveness, and embrace. Peacemaking is the work of family.

Our heavenly Father is not a peacekeeper; he is a peacemaker.

God wants to make peace with us, in us, and between us. When Gideon meets the angel of the LORD, he is sure he will perish. The LORD, however, brings peace, not woe: "Peace be to you." In awe, Gideon builds an altar naming it, "The LORD is Peace" (Judges 6:23–24). When the disciples are surprised by the resurrected Jesus in their fearful hiding, Jesus's words are "Peace be with you" (John 20:19). When Paul reflects on what Jesus accomplished on the cross, he declares the great reality of inner peace: "Since we have been justified by faith, we have peace with God through our Lord Jesus

Christ" (Romans 5:1). When Paul describes what Jesus has wrought between Jews and Gentiles—the warring siblings—he says, "He himself is our peace, who has made us both one and broken down in his flesh the dividing wall of hostility" (Ephesians 2:14).

Jesus made peace and destroyed our hostility with those who are different or who disappoint or even damage us. The cross is a paradox: a cruel instrument redefined as a peacemaking symbol.

Our Father's heart is on his sleeve: "How good and pleasant it is when God's people live together in unity" (Psalm 133:1). Peace is our Father's will: peace with him, peace within, and peace between his kids.

Furthermore, God expects his children to bring his peace to his fractured world. We join his peacemaking work. The reason we need peace with God through Christ is because we cannot make peace we do not have. Peace is our Father's will, and it is the enviable life Christians have in Christ and that which we are to be happy to make.

The early church was instructed to "make every effort to do what leads to peace and mutual edification" (Romans 14:9). Peacemaking is a fruit of knowing God the Peacemaker. Peacemaking is God's everlasting good news applied to everyday life. This is where the gospel comes closest to home. Our feet are to wear the readiness that comes from the gospel of peace wherever we go (Ephesians 6:15).

Peacemaking is even a prerequisite for authentic Christian worship: "If you are offering your gift at the altar and there remember that your brother or sister has something against you, leave your gift there in front of the altar. First

go and be reconciled to them; then come and offer your gift"
(Matthew 5:23–24).

To be a child of God is to be at peace with the Father,
to be at peace within yourself, and to make peace the way
he does. To bring wholeness, tie broken things together, and
actively bring an end of whatever wars we can is God's family
business. This is the work of ambassadors of reconciliation
who are worthy of the title "children of God."

Slow down and consider: Where is peace shattered
around you? In your family car? With a colleague? With your
spouse? Is their conflict in your church or neighbourhood?
Are politics dividing and even killing people? Are we content
with avoidance, tolerance, and passivity, which only produce
fragile armistices? Our heavenly Father is a Peacemaker;
what is keeping you from moving beyond peacekeeping?

God ended the war.

In Christ, God has made a comprehensive, whole peace
for the world. It's what the angels announced at Jesus's birth:
"Glory to God in the highest heaven, and on earth peace to
those on whom his favour rests" (Luke 2:14). In Jesus Christ,
God reveals how peace is made: he joined the wounded (that's
us), named the wounds (Jesus exposes broken peace-less-ness),
forgave the offender (the cross a sign of how costly forgiveness
is), and built a common future (he speaks peace and says, "As
the Father has sent me, I am sending you" [John 20:21]).

The high honour of being called "children of God,"
peacemakers, comes at a high cost. Yet someone must
make peace, or else things don't just keep, they deteriorate.
So where must you join the wounded, name the wounds,
offer forgiveness, and work for a common future?

SIXTEEN

AMBASSADORS OF CHRIST: THE PERSECUTED

My friend grew up in a Christian family in the fading days of the Soviet Union. When she was eight years old, she was brought before school administration and asked if her parents *made* her go to church. Her mom had prepared her for such a moment. She could trust the Holy Spirit. She responded, "No, I *want* to go to church." Unbeknownst to her, if she had said her parents *made* her go to church, she would have been removed from her home and put into an orphanage.

Scripture reveals God as the Righteous One. He is right, does what is right, and commands what is right.

> He is the Rock, his works are perfect,
>> and all his ways are just.
>> A faithful God who does no wrong,
>> upright and just is he. (Deuteronomy 32:4)

> For the LORD is righteous;
>> he loves righteous deeds;
>> the upright shall behold his face. (Psalm 11:7 ESV)

> You are righteous, LORD,
>> and your laws are right.
>> The statutes you have laid down are righteous;
>> they are fully trustworthy. (Psalm 119:137–138)

The LORD is righteous in all his ways
and faithful in all he does." (Psalm 145:17)

"And there is no other God besides me,
A righteous God and a Savior." (Isaiah 45:21)

The Old Testament prophets present the disturbing paradox of righteousness: "Righteous are You, O Lord, that I would plead my case with You; indeed, I would discuss matters of justice with You: Why has the way of the wicked prospered? Why are all those who deal in treachery at ease?" (Jeremiah 12:1 NASB1995).

If Almighty God is righteous, why all the unrighteousness? Why are little children treated unjustly?

Jesus knew the righteousness of the Father. "Righteous Father, though the world does not know you, I know you" (John 17:25). Jesus's coming is right on time and reveals what is right. But righteousness—even God's right-ness revealed in Christ—is often hated and suffers injustice, like a little girl in a principal's office. Peter charges the religious leaders for this: "You disowned the Holy and Righteous One and asked that a murderer be released to you" (Acts 3:14). The blessed life is ours precisely because righteousness was despised and rejected.

To become like our Father is to hunger and thirst for his righteousness (Matthew 5:6). The blessed and enviable life has hunger pangs for righteousness in this world, which is a buffet of unrighteousness. Jesus says, "Blessed are those who are persecuted because of righteousness, for theirs is the kingdom of heaven. Blessed are you when people insult you, persecute you and falsely say all kinds of evil against you because of me. Rejoice and be glad, because great is your reward in heaven, for in the same way they persecuted the prophets who were before you" (Matthew 5:10–12).

The blessedness of the persecuted is their impending reward and carries prophetic power—a window into another world—when all that is unjust is revealed as unenviable, dark, and hopeless.

The first Christians embraced this. The apostles thought it a great honour to suffer for Jesus's sake (Acts 5:41). Peter instructs, "It is better, if it is God's will, to suffer for doing good than for doing evil" (1 Peter 3:17). Paul rejoiced in suffering for the sake of the churches (Colossians 1:24) and described the believer's honour: "It has been granted to you on behalf of Christ not only to believe in him, but also to suffer for him" (Philippians 1:29). "Theirs is the kingdom of heaven" is the same inheritance promised to the persecuted and the poor in spirit (Matthew 5:3). The poor and persecuted have been bequeathed the kingdom of God, carry a heavenly passport, and are a prophetic and powerful sign in a proud world.

Which life is the most blessed, enviable, and authoritative: the adult cornering the eight-year-old with political and ideological intent or the eight-year-old cornering the adult with innocent trust and goodness?

But there is a caveat. Peter said suffering for doing good is blessedness, refinement, and God-like (1 Peter 3:14–4:2); but suffering for being a bully, acting selfishly, or doing unjustly is warranted and nothing to brag about (1 Peter 2:19–21). Ambassadors of Jesus will share in the rejection he experienced for what is good, right, true, and just. The persecution of an ambassador is intended to make King Jesus shine and prophetically reveal the enviable life of God's kingdom.

The righteousness we thirst for in the world is to become the righteousness we joyfully endure hardship for. Suffering makes us a participant in the world's mourning. Blessed are persecuted ambassadors of Christ who don't seek suffering to make a point but seek the Righteous One to become *his* point of light in the world.

Slow down and consider: Do you know stories of persecution for Jesus's sake? What has been produced when people faithfully endure opposition for righteousness' sake? What do you observe to be the prophetic power of such witness? As Christ's ambassador, how are you choosing to suffer for righteousness' sake rather than participate in the unrighteousness around you?

SEVENTEEN

AMBASSADORS OF CHRIST: YOU ARE SALT AND LIGHT

My wife complains about my cooking because too often I don't use salt. "Make it live, for goodness' sake!" is what she's saying.

At night, our basement, where our children sleep, gets eerily dark. So we have small night-lights plugged in. It's amazing how those tiny bulbs make a big difference.

"You are the salt of the earth, but if the salt has lost its taste, how shall its saltiness be restored? It is no longer good for anything expect to be thrown out and trampled under people's feet. You are the light of the world. A city on a hill cannot be hidden. Nor do people light a lamp and put it under a basket, but on a stand, and it gives light to all in the house. In the same way, let your light shine before others, so that they may see your good works and give glory to your Father in heaven" (Matthew 5:13–16).

Jesus builds on the blessed life of his ambassadors with the effect of their enviable life: the God-centered, Christ-formed, Spirit-led blessed life *is* salt and light. Disciples— poor in spirit, mourning, meek, hungering and thirsting for righteousness, merciful, pure in heart, peacemakers, and persecuted—become *salt*, adding a heavenly flavour, and *light*, refusing to be hidden, and bringing glory to God.

Two salty Old Testament references are worth noting.

First, a woman who became a pillar of salt (Genesis 19:26). Lot and his wife were part of Abraham's clan, meant to be a blessing to the nations (Genesis 12:1–3), but life in Sodom and Gomorrah swept them away. They were mercifully given an opportunity to escape the destruction coming on their city ruined by wickedness (which Ezekiel 16:49–50 describes as not only sexual immorality, but pride, selfishness, and mercilessness—the opposite of the life described by the beatitudes). But Lot's wife looked back, and her life, meant to be a blessing to the nations, turned into a useless pillar of salt.

Second, Israel's grain offerings to God were always to be salted (Leviticus 2:13). God deserved what was flavourful, costly, and pure. Yahweh was to be honoured with the best; and that best became better with salt.

Jesus says his disciples are salt. His ambassadors are the additive bringing God honour. Ambassadors of Christ are not useless salt that has lost purpose, but salty presence, proclaiming God's glory in their world (Colossians 4:5–6). Christ's ambassador is an offering of purity and praise, knowing God's pleasing will (Romans 12:1–2).

And, says Jesus, we are light.

The LORD led his people from Egypt by a pillar of fire (Exodus 13:21). Psalm 44:3 sings that the promised land was granted to Israel by the light of God's presence. Isaiah declares that through his servant the LORD will reveal his ways as a light to the nations (Isaiah 51:4). So when Jesus says *he* is the light of the world (John 8:12), he reveals himself as the fulfilment of God's liberating presence and justice. And stunningly, he says his disciples are the light of the world too! We his ambassadors radiate his very own light.

Slow down and consider: Can you see places where the flavour of God needs to be added? Have you become useless in those places because your attention is turned elsewhere? Can you see where some light of heaven needs to shine? Does your presence illuminate? Is your presence a ray of God's hope?

Being salt and light is not about working harder; it is the effect of the blessed life that is the direct result of being called to, for, with, and by the glory of Jesus. By the power of the Spirit, Christ's ambassadors embody the character of God and *are* the salt of the earth and the light of the world. Your usefulness and illumination come from remaining with and in him. What's your plan for that today?

EIGHTEEN

AMBASSADORS OF CHRIST: YOU NEED THE HOLY SPIRIT

In my first summer job I did something irresponsible but managed to get away with it. A few "white lies" (if there are such things) covered up my negligence. No harm, no foul. At the end of the summer, I moved on and thought it was all behind me.

A few months later, however, I fully surrendered my life to Christ. As I submitted the nooks and crannies of my life to Jesus, I was hounded by that unreconciled relationship with my summer boss. Each day I passed that workplace and couldn't shake God's nagging until I went into my former employer's office to confess my negligence and deception. He was stunned. I was free.

Why was I so driven toward reconciliation?

The Old Testament law called for a guilt offering when an Israelite realized their sin in breaching a relationship in the community through deceit, robbery, or even finding something lost and lying about it (Leviticus 6:1–7). Unreconciled relationships in the community had to be addressed. In Matthew 5:23–24 Jesus says, "Therefore, if you are offering your gift at the altar and there remember that your brother or sister has something against you, leave your gift there in front of the altar. First go and be reconciled to them; then come and offer your gift." Jesus connects the act of worship with the life of worship. And, at the center of this wholeness that pleases God is reconciliation.

But how do we come to this remembrance at the altar? How did I come to the awareness of a breach in need of repair with my boss? The answer is the person of the Holy Spirit.

The Holy Spirit is always seeking to make whole what has shattered and is the essential engine counselling humanity towards the ministry of reconciliation.

As ambassadors of Christ's reconciling work, we cannot depend on our own strength, intelligence, or even best practices. Those matter, but only to the extent that we are filled with and surrendered to the leading of the Spirit of God. Our own power and ability will deceive us and let us down.

Jesus's declaration of his reconciling and liberating ministry in the world was prompted by the Spirit (Luke 4:18–21). Jesus said the Spirit would dwell with and within believers (John 14:16–17). Jesus said the Spirit's coming would awaken the awareness of sin that destroys the world (John 16:8–11). The Holy Spirit would guide believers when the world turns on them (Luke 12:11–12) and puts the witness to the reconciling work of God in Christ under pressure (John 15:26–27). When Jesus breathed the Holy Spirit on his disciples, it was specifically connected to the arrival of his peace and the authority to be a community of forgiveness (John 20:21–23). When the Spirit was given to the church on the day of Pentecost, he immediately brought diverse peoples together into a reconciled community (Acts 2:11). Paul declares that Christians are to contend for the unity of the Spirit in the bond of peace (Ephesians 4:1–6).

Can you see? The Spirit is like a sheepdog herding disciples toward wholeness and provides the power to live out God's reconciling work.

Jesus's teaching on the Spirit in John 14–16 begins with his disciples' desire to understand more about the Father's ways. Do you desire his ways? Have you told God that desire? We must ask and then receive what he brings our way. If we desire, ask, and receive what the Spirit is seeking, we will be more whole and can expect Spirit-led opportunities to participate in God's plan to wipe away every tear and eliminate all that destroys the wholeness God intended and will fully restore (Revelation 21:3–5).

Slow down and consider: Is there any relationship or situation coming to mind right now in need of courageous reconciling? Might that be the Holy Spirit's strong nudge? And if the Spirit of God is prompting, then the Spirit will also give the power to turn and do what leads to righteousness, wholeness, and witness of Jesus. The Spirit will direct your steps. Your job is not to control the outcome—your responsibility is obedience. The same Spirit who raised Jesus from the dead and reconciled us to God (Romans 8:9–11) is the same Spirit who is alive in you and in your church. How will you follow his reconciling lead today?

NINETEEN

AMBASSADORS OF CHRIST: YOU NEED THE KINGDOM OF GOD

In 2010, a member the Colville Confederated Tribes in Washington State, USA, crossed into Canada and shot an elk. He was charged with hunting without a licence in British Columbia. The man, however, claimed he had an Aboriginal right to hunt across borders because his people's ancestral territory had always extended into what today is Canada. The Supreme Court of Canada eventually agreed, declaring that "groups whose members are neither citizens nor residents of Canada can be Aboriginal peoples of Canada." In other words, the elk hunter has an identity bigger than and not defined by the arbitrary Canada–USA border established by the Oregon Treaty in 1846.

This battle for hunting rights is a window into one of the most important understandings for ambassadors of Christ: your identity is defined not by your flag but by your faith. When you surrender your life to Jesus and his leadership, you are gloriously rescued from the kingdom of darkness, the kingdom of this world, and brought into the kingdom of light (Colossians 1:13; 1 Peter 2:9–10). This holy nation is borderless and timeless, "a great multitude that no one [can] count, from every nation, tribe, people and language, standing before the throne and before the Lamb" (Revelation 7:9).

"The time has come," Jesus came proclaiming. "The kingdom of God has come near. Repent and believe the good news!" (Mark 1:15). His invitation is to turn from all other allegiances—that's what repentance means—and stake your life and living—that's what believing means—on God's rulership that has always existed but is now brought up close and personal in Jesus Christ. With the arrival of the King, the Messiah and Saviour of the world, all other flags lower, and before his throne all crowns are laid down (Revelation 4:10).

Citizenship in God's kingdom is a very big deal. Jesus taught us to make the arrival of the Father's kingdom our prayer focus: "your kingdom come, your will be done, on earth as it is in heaven" (Matthew 6:10). Receiving the commission of kingdom ambassadorship is not for the faint of heart.

Jesus prayed for us: "My prayer is not that you take them out of the world but that you protect them from the evil one. They are not of the world, even as I am not of it" (John 17:15–16). And, before the political powers at his trial Jesus declared, "My kingdom is not of this world. If it were, my servants would fight to prevent my arrest by the Jewish leaders. But now my kingdom is from another place" (John 18:36).

Christians are first and foremost citizens of the kingdom of God. You *need* this kingdom. The world *needs* this kingdom of truth and light. This is your true citizenship and renewed indigeneity as a child of God. The values of God's kingdom are what you are to embody and represent as an ambassador of Christ. It is to this kingdom that the King is reconciling the world.

Slow down and consider: The elk hunter knew his identity was not defined by arbitrary borders, but by a bigger story. How aware are you of the bigger story you are part of as a follower of the King of kings? Consider your actions and allegiances. Consider what you cheer for. Consider what you pray for. Consider what you fight for. Consider what you are willing to lay down your life for. Are God's kingdom and his righteousness your main pursuit and identity?

The peoples of the world and the borders they draw continue to shift. In the time you have, in the place and among the people where God has rooted and sent you, you are an ambassador of another world. How is the Spirit inviting you to assess your allegiances? How might you be the answer to the prayer for the kingdom to come on earth just as it is in heaven today?

TWENTY

AMBASSADORS OF CHRIST:
YOU NEED TO PRAY

I have friends in volatile places. When I hear of the crises they are enduring, I'll ask what they need. They never ask for money, but they do ask for prayer.

The second-century Christian apologist, Aristides of Athens, writing when Christians were deemed suspicious, wrote, "The world stands by reason of the intercession of Christians." Clement of Alexandria, also in the second century, said, "(Prayer) is the only good force, to force God and to seize life from God."

Ambassadors of Christ need to pray. Disciples do not grow without prayer. Christian unity is not maintained without prayer. The world is not transformed without prayer. The world crumbles without prayer. Prayerfulness is, not surprisingly, a dominant theme throughout Scripture and seen constantly in the life of Jesus, our King.

Jesus modeled a life of prayer. He survived on dependent, conversational friendship with God the Father. The disciples witnessed this prayer-dependence in Jesus's life and hungered for it. "One day Jesus was praying in a certain place. When he finished, one of his disciples said to him, 'Lord, teach us to pray'" (Luke 11:1).

Jesus spoke about prayer with his disciples a lot. He told a parable of a persistent widow who badgered a judge for justice until he caved, holding up incessant bothering as the kind of praying God likes. Jesus taught we "should always pray and not give up" (Luke 18:1). Jesus implied bothersome praying that leads to what is just in the world is the type of faith he'll look for when he returns: "However, when the Son of Man comes, will he find faith on the earth?" (Luke 18:8). Faithful ambassadorial prayer—communication with God in heaven for his will to be done on earth (Matthew 6:9–13)—is Jesus's expectation.

Jesus made bold promises about corporate prayer. "Again, truly I tell you that if two of you on earth agree about anything they ask for, it will be done for them by my Father in heaven" (Matthew 18:19). The condition for this amazing promise is right relationships between his followers. It's not just that we agree on the request; it's that we are in harmony with one another. Reconciliation releases transformative prayer.

Elsewhere Jesus says, "You may ask me for anything in my name, and I will do it" (John 14:14). The condition for this powerful promise is a community believing in Jesus's divine identity and in right family relationship with God. Great promises are connected to unified, believing prayer. The life of a godly community produces powerful and effective praying (James 5:16).

The disciples learned these lessons and were devoted to prayer (Acts 2:42). It was their first response when the world was chaotic (Acts 4:23–31). They were joyfully surprised by answered prayer (Acts 12:12–17). Prayer led them into danger—such as when Ananias of Damascus heard Jesus ask him to go to a persecutor named Saul (Acts 9:10–17). Prayer led a storm-threatened ship out of danger—grounding Paul's sure belief that not one soul would be lost on the raging sea (Acts 27:21–26). Prayer was the source of mission and the advance of God's kingdom (Acts 16:6–10; Ephesians 6:18–20). Prayer is what Christians keep at when the world doesn't make sense, when answers are long in coming, and even when the answers are beyond life in this world (Revelation 6:9–11).

Prayer is the work of Christ's ambassadors.

Slow down and consider: What needs transforming in your life, friendships, household, church or society? What global calamity has captured your attention? The Bible and Christian history testify that nothing will begin to look and smell like heaven, that hope and reconciliation will remain distant, without ambassadorial prayer.

How are you developing a habit of prayer? Why not begin with the Lord's Prayer each day (Matthew 6:9–13)? Why not set phone alarms to call you to chat with your heavenly Father throughout the day? Why not commit to prayer with others—like your spouse or other disciples? God needs his ambassadors to pester heaven's headquarters habitually and regularly so that his kingdom advances on earth.

TWENTY-ONE

AMBASSADORS OF CHRIST: YOU NEED THE CHURCH

In response to the COVID-19 pandemic, people everywhere—including churches—stopped meeting as they once did. This abruptly shifted rhythms Christians had been used to. For some this was the first time in their lives that they could not "go to church." The church was closed. Or was it? The absence of the opportunity to go to a church building stirred an underlying deeper, more fundamental question. What is church anyway? Why does church matter? Is the church necessary?

Jesus made this profound declaration: "I will build my church, and the gates of Hades will not overcome it" (Matthew 16:18). Does this mission statement sound like your experience of church?

Jesus did not have most current conceptions of "church" in mind when he said this. The Greek word translated "church" is *ekklesia*. In the ancient world, *ekklesia* was about unity, responsibility, and activity. The word described those called out from their community to take responsibility for their community. It was an assembly chosen—somewhat like a municipal council today—to assume care and stewardship of the place they lived.

Ekklesia was not a place you went to; it was something you were. It was a chosen people with purpose, responsibility, and mission serving with the authority to seek the common good and flourishing of the population and place.

Jesus's Matthew 16 declaration about the church he is building was in response to Peter's confession that Jesus was the Messiah, the Son of the living God (Matthew 16:16). Those who see Jesus clearly, who know him as the true King, are called out of their time and place, gathered by God's grace and choosing, and being built by Jesus as those responsible for the advance of heaven against the gates of hell.

In ancient cities the gates were where authoritative decisions for the city were made. The decisions and directions of the powers of hell and darkness that are impacting real places need to be reconciled to God's purposes so that true flourishing under the reign of God can return. The wholeness of God's *shalom* must prevail. This is what the church, the *ekklesia* Jesus is building, is to be and do!

The church is an embassy, a community of God's kingdom ambassadors. In the New Testament, the *ekklesia* has a marvelous purpose: "His intent was that now, through the church, the manifold wisdom of God should be made known to the rulers and authorities in the heavenly realms, according to his eternal purpose that he accomplished in Christ Jesus our Lord" (Ephesians 3:10–11). The Bible's description of how the church advances God's eternal wisdom against the gates of hell can be described in these ways:

- Proclaiming the good news of God's kingdom and the lordship of Jesus Christ.
- Teaching, baptizing, and nurturing new believers in their identity in Christ.

- Responding to human need through loving service, hospitality, and generosity.
- Transforming injustice, violence, and oppression, and being peacemakers and reconcilers.
- Stewarding the health of creation.

Ambassadors of Christ are about this purpose, which is God's mission in history. You have been brought into God's family and gifted by your Creator with natural gifts and by the Spirit with special gifts for this holy purpose! You are an essential part of the church Jesus is still building!

Slow down and consider: Would this kind of church ever be closed? Can you see why you and the world need the *ekklesia*? Can you see why your local church needs you? How is Jesus's vision of the church grander than simply attending a service? Can you see why this kind of people with this kind of calling is so necessary today?

What awakens in you as you consider these things? Have you surrendered your ambassadorial responsibility within the embassy? Are you a spectator? How might you help your local church more faithfully? How might you encourage and strengthen the believers you are in communion with? How do you see Jesus building his church now that you should celebrate?

TWENTY-TWO

AMBASSADORS OF CHRIST: YOU NEED THE POWER OF FORGIVENESS

I went through a painful relational mess with another Christian. Neither of us intentionally hurt the other, but our decisions, strengths, and personalities clashed and conflicted. Both could claim being right, and both of us were also wrong. The irony—and challenge—was that we were both in Christian ministry, seeking to lead people to Christlikeness. How could we authentically serve Jesus if we were not willing to reconcile and forgive?

If we think we know what it is to be wronged, consider God. God is the most offended and sinned against Being there is. A child can deeply wound a parent as no one else can. Lying to our parents or taking advantage of their love is grievous. We've all been guilty of that to some degree or know how it feels. So consider what our heavenly Father is confronted by routinely—and yet, God is *the* forgiver.

Scripture teems with the power of forgiveness that is inherent to God's nature. "He passed in front of Moses, proclaiming, 'The LORD, the LORD, the compassionate and gracious God, slow to anger, abounding in love and faithfulness, maintaining love to thousands, and forgiving wickedness, rebellion and sin. Yet he does not leave the guilty unpunished; he punishes the children and their children for the sin of the parents to the third and fourth generation'" (Exodus 34:6–7).

"If my people, who are called by my name, will humble themselves and pray and seek my face and turn from their wicked ways, then I will hear from heaven, and I will forgive their sin and will heal their land" (2 Chronicles 7:14).

"You, LORD, are forgiving and good, abounding in love to all who call to you" (Psalm 86:5).

God is a scandalous forgiver. It is almost unjust that God forgives! If anyone has reason to withhold forgiveness, it is the Creator who breathed us life only to receive our blatant snubbing, disobedience, and rejection. Still, God actively longs to forgive. God searches for reason to have mercy. From Cain's treachery to the sacrificial system for Israel, God's currency is mercy and forgiveness. It will not be his wrath (as justified as it is) but kindness that proves powerful enough to move us to turn and join him as his ambassadors in a world of offense and sin (Romans 2:4).

"If you, LORD, kept a record of sins, LORD, who could stand? But with you there is forgiveness, so that we can, with reverence, serve you" (Psalm 130:3–4).

Forgiveness is not cheap. God bore the enormous cost forgiving requires and demands. Jesus's innocent broken body on the cross is what makes forgiveness possible. He is the Lamb of God who takes away the sin of the world (John 1:29; Revelation 5:9–10). Forgiveness requires powerful, selfless love. Christians celebrate this costly love at the Lord's table: "This is my blood of the covenant, which is poured out for many for the forgiveness of sins" (Matthew 26:28).

Through the humility of repentance and coming home to the Father, we find forgiveness, the restoration of relationship, and are commissioned into God's movement of forgiveness that transforms relationships and societies. This, too, is not cheap.

Ambassadors of Christ pray together for forgiveness, "Forgive us our debts, as we also have forgiven our debtors" (Matthew 6:12). Forgiveness is a serious and central business in God's eyes. Confronted by the great forgiveness of God and the call to be like him in the parable of the unmerciful servant, those who refuse to offer forgiveness stand exposed and punished before the merciful master: "This is how my heavenly Father will treat each of you unless you forgive your brother or sister from your heart" (Matthew 28:35).

Forgiveness is Christian duty, and the Holy Spirit instills the power of forgiveness: "Receive the Holy Spirit. If you forgive anyone's sins, their sins are forgiven; if you do not forgive them, they are not forgiven" (John 20:22–23). Ambassadors of Christ are empowered as brokers of forgiveness and restoration.

With all this good news, how could I resist the journey of forgiveness with my brother in Christ? We worked at it. It took time. Eventually we forgave one another and embraced. We even washed one another's feet. We found new freedom and power.

Slow down and consider: How big was—or is—the pile of "stuff" you need forgiveness for? In Christ there is the forgiveness of sins. In Christ we are made right with God. No more condemnation (Romans 8:1). Period. Pause and worship.

Then pay attention to any relationships (past or present) where you harbour offense and unforgiveness. Are you applying the same power of forgiveness in those relationships that you have experienced from your heavenly Father? What practical steps toward forgiveness are needed? Are you as diligent at forgiving as you are at coddling the wound or offense? Where do you have opportunity as an ambassador of Christ to participate in the power of forgiveness?

TWENTY-THREE

AMBASSADORS OF CHRIST: YOU NEED THE HEALING OF MEMORIES

Do you remember my dad crying? When I saw him in tears, it left a mark. The family farm he grew up on was being auctioned, and the clan had gathered to prepare things for sale. Something triggered a powerful memory in my dad that made him a blubbering mess in front of me. I still wonder if that memory impacted the way my dad fathered me.

There are memories in our lives, and in peoples and nations, that are carried for years. Painful pasts, sins against us, and sins we have committed don't just disappear. Memories linger and eventually overflow the carefully manicured banks of the rivers of our lives and flood those around us with the unreconciled muck of the past. Memories of what was inflicted between French and English, settlers and First Nations, Germans and Jews, Hutus and Tutsis, Crusaders and Muslims, Muslims and Yazidis, Protestants and Catholics, by one town to another, one family to another, or one sibling to another don't just evaporate. Memories percolate.

Time does not heal all wounds. Time can, in fact, make them fester like a deep infection, oozing out resentment and twisted tales that get passed along, entangling the next generation in the thorns of the past. Unhealed memories erupt into destructive conflicts among nations. Unhealed memories produce ineffective ambassadors of Christ who are to join God's healing of those nations.

Our memories need God's healing.

Scripture addresses a painful memory between brothers. Cain kills Abel. Cain is aware others will not forget what he has done. Even though there are consequences for Cain's wickedness, he is marked to ensure that though people may bear a grudge, God marks the memory with the scandal of grace (Genesis 4:15). God is different.

God's promise to Abraham to bless all nations through him was a healing of the memory of curse that has beset us all east of Eden (Genesis 12:1–3). When the Hebrews cried out because all they could remember was slavery, it was God who "remembered his covenant with Abraham, Isaac and Jacob" (Exodus 2:24). The exodus and deliverance of the Israelites from Egypt was marked by Passover, a distinct new memory-making ritual for those who were not only free from the woes of slavery but free to relive annually the need never to return to that identity.

God remembers differently than we do. We remember trauma. We return to our past like a dog to its vomit (Proverbs 26:11). We act and live out of regrets and wounds that we or our people have experienced. God, conversely, remembers covenant. God, astoundingly, forgets sin (Isaiah 43:25)!

The cross of Jesus Christ is the climax and clincher of all this. Jesus said his blood spilled traumatically on the cross is the new covenant for many, and at the Lord's table we have a new memory-making ritual (Matthew 26:28). Forgiveness and the healing of memories are inseparable. We need freedom from sin, but we also need freedom from the memories of the old identities, wounds, generational sins, and lies that shaped us. We need the memories of sins and slaveries healed.

God forgives and remembers our sins no more (Hebrews 8:12), but we humans don't so easily forget. We tell stories and erect monuments about wounds long past and forget what we should celebrate. When our memories remain unreconciled, we easily repeat our tragic and treasonous pasts—crusading as those carrying the cross of forgiveness while slaughtering our enemies because the present is stirring up past wounds and fears, like a stick muddying the waters of what we thought was a clear-flowing stream.

Slow down and consider: What memory makes you cry, run, or get angry? What unhealthy, unreconciled memories do you drag around like a heavy backpack? How are those memories impacting you, others, and your people?

Healing memories requires trusting the Holy Spirit's leading. It requires naming and telling the truth about memories we cling to. It requires courage to wade into relationships with those we wounded or who wounded us or who represent the wound. It means applying the forgiveness won for us by Christ to our past so we can freely run forward—as Peter had to do after the resurrection, when he walked with Jesus into his painful memories of denial and cowardice (John 21:15–23). It demands we do justly—righting or restoring what remains broken through prayer and acts of love, restitution, and sacrifice.

This is not easy. Our memories can be scary places we avoid. We will probably need help as we stumble forward. Are you eager to at least take the smallest step? The ambassador of Christ as a minister of reconciliation must go there.

TWENTY-FOUR

AMBASSADORS OF CHRIST: YOU NEED THE HELP OF OTHERS

Just before I turned forty my family moved across the country. In a new location, I found it surprisingly difficult to decide who should be invited to my fortieth celebration. A few months later, we experienced a very challenging family crisis which revealed a similar challenge: who is it that I invite into my struggles when I don't know people very well? Who travels with you through life's celebrations and struggles?

Ambassadors of Christ are sent into a world in need of reconciliation, but we are all human. To be healthy—walking through our wounds, past, and memories—requires not going alone. We need circles of care to help us become more whole.

In God himself we see a circle of care. In the triune Oneness of Father, Son, and Spirit, we know a God not only ministering to the world, but God ministering to himself. The wonderful mystery is that God is One but not alone. Scripture begins with a divine conversation: "Then God said, 'Let us make mankind in our image, in our likeness'" (Genesis 1:26). God's plan for his creation is the spillover of mutuality and unity. We are made in the image of this unified, eternal, good circle of love and care.

This God who is "one for all and all for one" is seen in the baptism of Jesus. "Just as Jesus was coming up out of the water, he saw heaven being torn open and the Spirit descending on him like a dove. And a voice came from heaven: 'You are my Son, whom I love; with you I am well pleased'" (Mark 1:10–11). The Holy One is seen and heard in healthy and holy self-interest for the sake of reconciling the world. Jesus is on no solo mission. He is well cared for by Father and Spirit.

This community of care found in God is then embodied in the body of Christ. The church is a circle of care. The gifts of the Holy Spirit are given to create a healthy unity of care. Prophecy, serving, teaching, generosity, leading, and doing acts of mercy help us toward wholeness (Romans 12:6–8). Receiving the strengths of others contributes to our own flourishing, and we contribute to theirs.

The love of God, of course, binds this all together (1 Corinthians 13). Putting into action the love for God and neighbour—those we are to love as ourselves (Leviticus 19:18; Matthew 22:37–39)—the apostle Paul instructs Christians to put on compassion, kindness, and humility as we bear with one another and forgive one another, as God's word dwells in us and overflows in teaching and admonishing one another into the life ruled by the peace of Christ (Colossians 3:12–17). The church is the visible reality of the circle of care found in God himself.

Slow down and consider: Who is it that you call to celebrate with or help in times of struggle? Do you have a circle of care, or are you a lonely ambassador? Who is it that you turn to, to help heal memories or instruct you, to walk through the journey of forgiveness or pray with you? Who makes that list? Who has the gifts?

It's helpful to think about the circles of care described by those caring for workers on the frontlines of intercultural activity globally. Picture it this way (as used by Multiply, a global mission agency):

> At the core is Master Care; the presence and ministry of God the Father, Son, and Holy Spirit. We start with God, our Good Master, and His good news. We go first to Him and His Word to address our joys and sorrows, listening for and receiving the Spirit's comfort and correction.
>
> The second circle is Self and Mutual Care. We give attention to personal spiritual practices and a church family who know and love us. We need spiritual friends. We need people who mourn and rejoice with us, speak truth to us, and are long-haul companions and spurs in the practice of the love of God.
>
> The third circle is Ministries and Programs. We need systems and structures, courses and organized methods that help us in specific expertise and wisdom. We need people who can teach and lead us to new awakenings, skills, and action.
>
> Finally, we may need a circle of Specialized Care. Sometimes we need people like counselors, therapists, doctors, or spiritual directors who can help us process painful realities and experiences.

Ambassadors of Christ cannot go it alone. But here's the thing: sometimes we begin with the last of these circles—specialized care—when we should begin with the Master.

We sometimes rely on professionals without having spiritual friendships or personal discipleship practices. Sometimes we expect a program or a course to fix us when that's only a slice of what we need.

So are you going alone? Are you starting from the core? What do you need now in each of these circles of care? How are you contributing to the wholeness of others? Is there a birthday party you should be attending or initiating?

TWENTY-FIVE

AMBASSADORS OF CHRIST: JOIN THE PEOPLE

I joined an ice hockey league for old-timers and wannabes. Leagues like these end up being as much about the beer as the game so some guys were quite surprised when I, the local pastor, signed up. They were even more surprised when they discovered I could play and not hurt the team's chance of winning. My local credibility grew as I embraced the late-night sport and banter.

Then tragedy struck. A player committed suicide. It rocked everyone. Few had a foundation of faith to stand on. Another Christian brother and I were asked to host postgame conversations to help process and reconcile the grief and pain. This would never have happened had we not joined the people.

God joins us. In all of life's unreconciled and unresolved questions and complexities, God comes near. Adam and Eve upend the apple cart, and sin rushes into the human story— but God joins them, walking in the garden seeking them. It is they who hide, not the Creator (Genesis 3:8). Cain slays Abel, but God joins him to address head-on what is broken. It is Cain who leaves the presence of the LORD (Genesis 4:9–16), not the LORD who abandons him. Childless Abram and Sarai take things into their own hands to produce an heir. Ishmael is born to Hagar, Sarai's maidservant, and unsurprisingly this erupts into domestic discord. Hagar flees to the wilderness, but the LORD joins her there (Genesis 16:1–16; 21:8–21). God joins the messy lives of Cain and Hagar, yet neither is central in God's larger plan to bring redemption and reconciliation to the world.

And that's a wonderful thought: God joins people wherever there is mess, from the most undeserving, like Cain to the rejected, like Hagar. With holy purpose the Bible focuses in on Cain's other brother, Seth (Genesis 4:25–5:8), and Sarai's miracle child, Isaac (Genesis 17:15–21), but we repeatedly see God joining humanity in our unreconciled realities. God is Emmanuel—God with us (Isaiah 7:14).

Emmanuel is ultimately revealed in Jesus Christ, the Messiah born through the line of Isaac and Seth (Luke 3:34–38). In Christ God dwells among us and reveals his glory (John 1:14). Jesus gloriously, and often scandalously, joined the people. He joined those whom the descendants of Abraham thought he shouldn't, like tax collectors and prostitutes (Mark 2:15–17; Luke 7:36–50; 19:1–10). People scoffed at this, but God had always joined the Cains and Hagars, so why not hang out with Zacchaeus (Luke 19:1–10) or let a woman dry his feet with her hair (John 12:3)? Jesus didn't join their activity; he accompanied their humanity. God joins those made in his image. How else will we who are sick or lost find our way home and become participants in his justice and righteousness?

Slow down and consider: Where is there unresolved and unreconciled mess around you? Is it in your own story? Jesus joins you. Are you aware of his presence? Has he sent someone your way to embody his presence? Who are the jerks like Cain or the mistreated like Hagar that Jesus may be sending you to come alongside?

Ambassadors of Christ must grow in spiritual depth and godly character if they are to join the wounding and wounded as reconcilers and be vessels of God's holy presence. We are to join others as God joined us, with grace and truth (John 1:14). We join humanity with conviction, compassion, and humility. We come alongside in Jesus's costly way; after all, that is the way he joined us.

Pray with eyes wide open. Who is it that God is leading you to join? Then, giving time, living consistently, and rooted deeply in God's character growing in you, join the unresolved and unreconciled places, like beer leagues, as a minister of reconciliation.

TWENTY-SIX

AMBASSADORS OF CHRIST: EARN TRUST

In 2020, war erupted between Azerbaijan and Armenia in the landlocked South Caucasus region of Nagorno-Karabakh. A historically disputed area, the conflict was the spillover of pent-up past grievances, displacing and traumatizing thousands. Christians from other parts of the world sent aid. Once the conflict died down, authorities recognized that emotional and spiritual support for the suffering was needed. Who could they turn to for help?

They asked those who had earned trust through their sacrificial giving and acts of love. They asked if Christians could help with trauma counseling.

Abraham's living, bold trust in God was why God counted him righteous (Genesis 15:6). A living, bold reliance on God's unlimited trustworthiness is what the apostle Paul calls for: "To the one who does not work but trusts God who justifies the ungodly, their faith is credited as righteousness" (Romans 4:5). Trusting your feeble work and way is fleeting and futile. Trusting God is righteousness. But can God be trusted? Perhaps that is the larger question.

God is exceedingly trustworthy. God says what he does and does what he says. God is a covenant-maker and a covenant-keeper. God keeps promises. In his dealing with the unresolved and unreconciled realities of the world, God acts to earn our trust. Abraham's bold trust in God was not blind.

God had proven himself faithful since calling Abram to leave his people (Genesis 12:1–3), and so the weathered Chaldean could fully trust the LORD's promise to give him descendants as numerous as the stars despite being childless (Genesis 15:1–6). God earns trust, and this, like food and shelter given to the displaced in a war-torn land, leads to greater and deeper possibilities for healing and transformation.

Jesus came earning trust. Jesus's integrity and congruency of words and acts earned a bold trust that awakened a bold trust in God's grace. The fishermen who followed Jesus had cast nets unsuccessfully, but they trusted the carpenter's word and brought in a haul. Peter's response? "Go away from me, Lord; I am a sinful man!" (Luke 5:8).

As Jesus's way became more disruptive and the crowds began abandoning him, he asked his closest friends if they had lost confidence too. Again, it was Peter who responded, "Lord, to whom shall we go? You have the words of eternal life" (John 6:68). He could be trusted because his acts, in keeping with the promise-keeping God, were trust-building. When his opponents recoiled as Jesus controversially revealed himself as God (John 10:33), Jesus said, "Even though you do not believe me, believe the works, that you may know and understand that the Father is in me, and I in the Father" (John 10:38).

Jesus's works earned trust, even when his words were incomprehensible and even reprehensible. Even when rejected and nailed to a cross, Jesus remained trustworthy and faithful to the promises of God to the very end. We can trust Jesus because he went to and stayed on that cross (Matthew 26:53–54). Jesus's way is to bring *shalom* by earning trust.

In the unresolved and unreconciled realities of lives, communities, and even war zones, ambassadors of Christ must earn trust, which opens doors for wholeness and transformation.

Slow down and consider: Where is the Holy Spirit giving you eyes to see what needs wholeness and transformation? Are you trusted there? Or are you deemed suspicious? Can you simply ride in and save the day with words—even holy words? Is that Jesus's way? How is God asking you to stay with the people and earn trust? What will be the posture, price, and pace of such godly trust-building? And if trust is shaky and eroded, what is required of you to restore it?

TWENTY-SEVEN

AMBASSADORS OF CHRIST: TALK ABOUT LIFE

You pay to be on an airplane only to be surprised by the person you are eating with or even sleeping beside. This forced confinement can lead to interesting conversations and curiosity of the unknown. "Where are you from?" "Where are you going?" Not everyone likes this, but fascinating conversations about life can emerge with a stranger we are buckled beside and may need to crawl over at some point!

God is a talker. In the very beginning, Genesis repeats over and over, "And God said" (Genesis 1:3, 6, 9, etc.). Our creation in his image is the result of God speaking (Genesis 1:26), so perhaps it's not surprising that we like to talk too.

Repeatedly in Scripture God shockingly enters the social space of human beings and, like a talker on an airplane, initiates conversation. He spoke with Adam and Eve in Eden (Genesis 2–3), with Cain after he disposed of his brother (Genesis 4), with Abram (Genesis 12), with Moses as he chased his flocks (Exodus 3), and with Mary who received the news of an unlikely pregnancy (Luke 1:28). The Scriptures reveal repeatedly that God revels in conversation.

God also brings us into conversation with others. God's unseen hand often leads us into social spaces—like airplanes, cafés, and community halls—where talking about life is a precursor to building flourishing lives where the LORD's *shalom* can enter. God's ways of getting us to talk together are sometimes uncomfortable or unexpected—like tragedies and crises. Joseph's unplanned sojourns in Potiphar's house and Pharoah's prison led to serendipitous conversations that changed history (Genesis 39–40). Nehemiah could converse with the king because exile forced his people from their homeland (Nehemiah 2). Esther could banquet with the king and her people's archenemy because of God's silent leading (Esther 7).

We should not be surprised, therefore, that the Messiah came as a talker. He talked about life everywhere he went—in enemy territory (John 4), with a swindling tax collector (Luke 19:1–10), and, even in suffering, a Roman governor and a thief on a cross (Luke 23). He also formed a social network of twelve who were brought together to talk about life—which often exposed selfishness, lack of *shalom,* and the need to mature as those who would become his ambassador of reconciliation (Mark 9:33–37).

God is always at work by his Spirit to draw us into conversation with himself and others for his reconciling purposes.

Slow down and consider: Has God been trying to talk with you? Have you avoided or tuned out your Creator's voice? He longs to converse about wholeness and *shalom.* Has Jesus been leading you into unlikely conversation with someone? It will be for wholeness and *shalom.* Are you talking about real life with people or just the weather or headlines? Are you curious about the life story of those precious ones God brings your way? Are you avoiding the hard conversations? Are you silent when you should talk?

Not every conversation will be the equivalent of Jesus with Zacchaeus or the apostle Paul with King Agrippa (Acts 26). But if God is a talker and his Spirit is at work to bring his people into kingdom conversations, then ambassadors of Christ should awaken to the real possibility of talk about life being God's strategy to plant seeds and harvest a future of *shalom*—even on a plane.

TWENTY-EIGHT

AMBASSADORS OF CHRIST: CONFRONT SINFUL LIVING

"C an we talk?"

Does that question feel confrontational?

Few people enjoy confrontation. It can make the stomach twirl. It can bring up past "stuff" or awaken pride. Offense and self-justification rise quickly, even if we're about to hear truth that is good for us. Confrontation is usually interpreted negatively, but is it always so? Wounds from a friend can be trusted, can't they (Proverbs 27:6)?

From the very beginning God confronts.

God confronts Adam and Eve. Their actions required it. Interestingly, in the account of Genesis 3 both the serpent and God confront by using questions. The serpent fakes compassionate concern and asks, "Did God actually say, 'You shall not eat of any tree in the garden?'" (Genesis 3:1). The confrontation seeks to undermine, confuse, and destroy the trusting relationship between humanity and the Creator.

When the LORD God comes searching, he too asks a question: "Who told you that you were naked? Have you eaten of the tree of which I commanded you not to eat" (Genesis 3:11)? God's confrontation seeks to undo the lie that God cannot be trusted and that we are somehow incomplete.

The devil is an accuser (Revelation 12:10) who confronts with lies to wreck wholeness and shatter *shalom*. God confronts truthfully to restore. In Genesis 3, God calls humanity to consider the credibility of the source. Satan's confrontation stirs confusion and self-reliance. God's confrontation goes straight to the heart of sinful living to set free from the grip of the serpent and restore God's best, his *shalom*.

Genesis 3 sets the trajectory for God's interaction with humanity. In the Old Testament, God repeatedly confronts that which is not his will. He confronts the builders of Babel, Pharaoh in Egypt, the Israelites when they grumble, the greed of Achan, the wickedness of Ninevah *and* of the preacher who told them they were wicked, and through the prophets calls out hypocrisy, injustice, and systemic evil.

Jesus came full of grace and truth (John 1:14).

He unabashedly calls us sinners who cannot save ourselves. With penetrating insight he exposes destructive, sinful ways of living. His indiscriminate grace and truth are evident in his interaction with the woman at the well, Zacchaeus in the tree, the woman caught in adultery, and the scoffing and hypocritical Pharisees. Jesus even calls Peter "Satan" for trying to dissuade him from the way of the cross (Matthew 16:23). Jesus's parables confront too. The parables of the unmerciful servant (Matthew 18:21–35) and the sheep and the goats (Matthew 25:31–46) are direct.

The Holy Spirit also confronts, convicting the world of sin, God's righteousness, and coming judgment, says Jesus (John 16:8). Jesus even confronts his own body, the church, exposing the corporate sinful, compromised living of five of the seven churches in Revelation 2–3 to restore relationship and mission.

The New Testament letters reveal Christian communities learning to practice what can be so difficult: confronting sinful living with grace and truth. Wherever the lie of the accuser has taken root and *shalom* is shattered, Christians lovingly speak truth and confront what is contrary to God's freedom, holiness, and peace. Galatians 6:1 calls those who live by the Spirit to confront sinful living for the sake of restoration. These practices build a persistent healthy and whole church life because ignoring sinful living wrecks lives, shatters *shalom*, destroys community, erodes society, and agrees with the accuser, who is a liar!

Slow down and consider: As an ambassador of reconciliation, you are called to truth-telling and freedom from sinful living. What fruit of sinful living should be truthfully addressed around you?

But be prepared: the Holy Spirit is looking at *your* life first. Jesus will confront *your* sinful living—and don't be surprised if that comes through another believer, spouse, co-worker, or even a child. What is the Spirit confronting in you? How do you respond when your sin is revealed? Do you receive it as freedom and good news? If you don't respond with humility when the plank in your own eye is exposed (Matthew 7:3–5), you cannot—and should not—be confronting others.

Having started with yourself, you can then turn to your local church. Jesus is constantly speaking truth to his people to free us from patterns of sinful living that undermine God's mission (1 Peter 4:17). Local churches are pleadingly confronted by Jesus, who stands at the door knocking (Revelation 3:20). Jesus's freedom and peace require naming and identifying what is off the mark in the Christian community.

And then the *ekklesia*, having received the gift of having sinful living confronted, is called to confront sinful patterns and behaviour in society that shatter God's *shalom*, God's best for all. Any truth-telling in society, however, will be shallow and rightfully dismissed if we have not first welcomed the personal and corporate confrontation of our sinful living as the good news of God.

Ambassador of reconciliation, how might the Spirit be seeking to confront you, your church, and your society?

TWENTY-NINE

AMBASSADORS OF CHRIST:
MAKE PEOPLE WHOLE

A group of men were meeting with a guy in his fifties who had just become a Christian. His life had been marked by mistakes, losses, and broken relationships. After a few weeks of discipleship, one of the men asked, "Hey, what difference has Jesus made in your life?" Without hesitation he blurted, "I finally know how to &#%!@?ing love!" The power of Christ, embodied in the love of Christian community, was not just teaching theological truths, but helping him move toward wholeness and bring wholeness.

God makes people whole.

Humanity was barred from Eden after our fall into the grip of sin lest we eat of the tree of life, forever seeking knowledge of good and evil and ultimate decisions devoid of a restored relationship with our Creator (Genesis 3:22). From that moment God begins to work out his plan laid before the foundation of the world to bring us into wholeness as the adopted children of God (Ephesians 1:4–16). And children are not raised to first be aware of some legal status but to be whole in every way: physically, emotionally, intellectually, socially, and spiritually.

God's nature and restoring plan, revealed beginning in the Old Testament, is about wholeness in all these dimensions: this is God's *shalom*. God's shalom-centered will is to form people through whom he will reveal himself and bless the nations with the wholeness they have received. The Law given to Israel formed a community spiritually alive in God's presence; caring for physical needs; intellectually stimulated toward truth; socially attentive to relationships, justice, foreigners, and even animals; and emotionally knowing peace and not fear.

Loving God and loving your neighbour as yourself summarized how to walk out God's *shalom* wholeness (Deuteronomy 6:4–7; Leviticus 19:18). When the prophets confronted Israel's sin, their lament was not only for disbelieving truths about God and trusting in idols, but for not living and working out God's wholeness. The prophets cried out when belief and behaviour became unhinged from one another. Isaiah declared that the LORD had turned his eyes away because goodness and justice were withheld from those most deprived of wholeness: the fatherless and widow (Isaiah 1:16–17).

When Jesus arrived, he announced a mission of making people whole (Luke 4:18–19). The wholeness of God's *shalom* and Jubilee is why he had come. Luke revealed Jesus *doing the truth* about God. Jesus delivered Mary Magdelene and others from demonic power. He socially and economically brought wholeness to Matthew and Zacchaeus—both tax collectors. He healed the sick. He multiplied loaves and fishes. A Roman collaborator and a Jewish zealot became part of his closest circle. Jesus's entire strategy is centered on making people and the communities they are part of whole.

In fact, Jesus's suffering is interpreted in this whole way by Peter, who places the righteousness won on the cross in the context of Christians bringing social wholeness in the political realm (1 Peter 2:11–25).

Slow down and consider: How have you, like that new brother in Christ, been made whole and brought to peace, *shalom*, and Jubilee by Jesus? How have others helped you become increasingly whole? Have you divorced your spiritual life from the social, physical, emotional, and intellectual parts of life? Are you a student of God's wholeness? Is the ministry of reconciliation through your church making people whole or creating religious consumers? Where are people, families, and systems in your community fractured, spiritually, relationally, socially, intellectually, or emotionally?

Ask God to teach you how to walk in his *shalom* wholeness. Actively follow the Spirit in applying the wholeness of the way of Jesus to the whole of life.

THIRTY

AMBASSADORS OF CHRIST: CALL PEOPLE TO FOLLOW JESUS

A sorrowful phone call informed me that my cousin, Wayne, had died unexpectedly. Wayne was not only a relative, but also instrumental in my discipleship. He had invested deeply in the youth of my home community, and when the Spirit got my attention through a family tragedy, it was Wayne who had put flesh on what God had been doing beneath the surface of my life. Wayne called me to follow Jesus.

We end where we began, with God calling people.

God called Adam and Eve in the garden of Eden. God called Abraham. God called for Moses's attention. God even called Israel as an entire nation out of Egypt (Hosea 11:1). God called judges like Deborah. God called foreigners like Ruth. God called kings like David and Hezekiah. God called prophets like Jeremiah. Psalm 95 pleaded with Israel to not harden their hearts, but to hear God's voice (95:7b–10). Sometimes God called miraculously and privately—as with Isaiah—and other times God he used the voice of another person—as when Samuel called David. God calls so that people, and peoples, follow him into his wholeness, into the fullness of the reconciled life and the restoration of his *shalom*. God calls to make whole people ambassadors of his *shalom*.

It makes complete sense, therefore, that Jesus was a rabbi. A rabbi called so that the disciple/learner would grow to embody the teaching and ways of their Master. "'Come, follow me,' Jesus said, 'and I will send you out to fish for people'" (Matthew 4:19). Jesus called for not only personal spiritual fulfilment but missional recruitment. Jesus called people for healing. He called people like Matthew so he could hang out with his kind of people (Matthew 9:10–12). He called people like Peter to a life that was costly (John 21:18–19).

Jesus's call is to take up your cross and follow (Matthew 16:24–26). The wholeness, the *shalom*, of God is to work through the dough of human life and society like yeast (Matthew 13:33) as people hear God the Caller and follow. The work of Christ's ambassadors is to keep calling people to follow Jesus, just as Wayne did. Jesus called Wayne, and Wayne called me to follow Jesus, and Jesus called me into his reconciling mission. What a beautiful divine-human tapestry!

Calling people to follow Jesus forms shalom-centered communities of the called. Paul emphasizes this: "We are therefore Christ's ambassadors, as though God were making his appeal through us. We implore you on Christ's behalf: be reconciled to God" (2 Corinthians 5:20). The ministry of reconciliation is a ministry of calling. Our attitudes call. Our posture with people calls. Our actions call. Our love for one another calls (John 13:35).

And, never to be forgotten, our voices call. In fact, the ministry of reconciliation will be incomplete without verbally calling people to follow the One who is the Reconciler, who makes us whole, confronts sinful living, addresses real life, earns trust, and joins us. Jesus seeks to call and commission a diverse host of ambassadors. Someone fitted with the readiness of the gospel of peace (Ephesians 6:15) must come proclaiming the good news that all who have strayed are to come home to the Father and be recommissioned as dignitaries of the kingdom of heaven (Romans 10:15)!

Slow down and consider: Have you noticed that calling happens all around you? People call you. You call others. You are called to follow what's on social media. Society calls you to conform. Advertising calls you to watch something, believe something, or buy something. We are beckoned and we beckon. Calling is what humans do, because we are made in the image of the Caller.

Have you heard the call of Jesus to follow him? The voice from heaven pleads for you to come out of Babylon, the fallen, corrupted ways of the world, which has lost *shalom*: "Come out of her, my people" (Revelation 18:4). Have you responded? Who or what is it that you are calling people to? Are you a Wayne in someone's life? Is your church calling your region to follow Jesus's way of justice and righteousness?

Ask the Holy Spirit to reveal those who need to be called to follow Jesus. Perhaps, like Paul the Jew with the Gentile Corinthians, God will send you as a caller to people in another place. Or, like James the brother of Jesus, perhaps it will be the people you grew up with. Then, embodying the qualities and activities we have considered in these readings, live ready to boldly call people to follow Jesus (1 Peter 3:15–16). This is part of the ambassadorial task you and your church have so that more and more follow the Lamb wherever he goes (Revelation 14:4).

Other Titles by Castle Quay Books

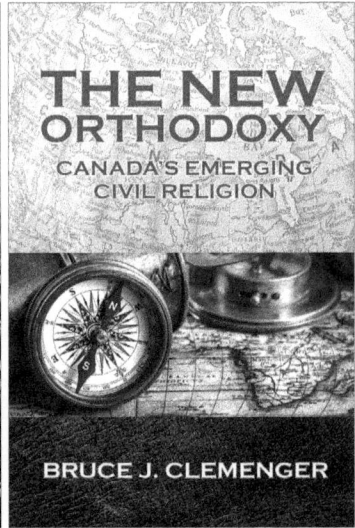

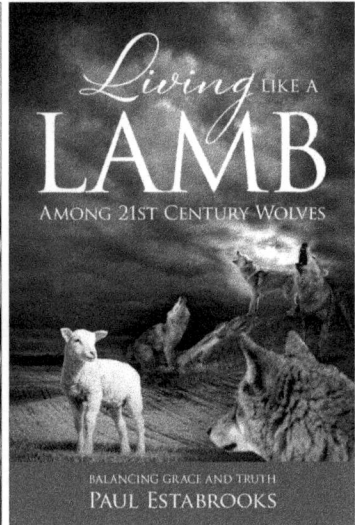

LIVE
YOUR ASSIGNMENT

Being Christ's Ambassador
in 7 Spheres of Life

PHIL M. WAGLER

THE NEW ORTHODOXY
CANADA'S EMERGING
CIVIL RELIGION

BRUCE J. CLEMENGER

UPDATED
AND REVISED
EDITION

LEADING ME
EIGHT PRACTICES OF A CHRISTIAN
LEADER'S MOST IMPORTANT ASSIGNMENT

"Imagine a treasure box for leaders with everything
you could possibly need in it..."
—from Foreword by Mark Buchanan

STEVE A. BROWN

Living LIKE A
LAMB
AMONG 21ST CENTURY WOLVES

BALANCING GRACE AND TRUTH
PAUL ESTABROOKS

Castle Quay Books

www.ingramcontent.com/pod-product-compliance
Lightning Source LLC
LaVergne TN
LVHW010318070426
835511LV00026B/3491